S & A Fletcher

THE RISK

THE RISK

Jenny Cooke

KINGSWAY PUBLICATIONS
EASTBOURNE

First published 1985

ISBN 0 86065 358 7

This is a true story. In certain cases names of individuals and minor details of their circumstances have been changed to protect their anonymity.

Front cover design by Vic Mitchell

Printed in Great Britain for
KINGSWAY PUBLICATIONS LTD
Lottbridge Drove, Eastbourne, E. Sussex BN23 6NT by
Cox & Wyman Ltd, Reading.
Typeset by Nuprint Services Ltd, Harpenden, Herts.

With deep love to my parents
who taught me never to give up
and
who have always stood by me.

Contents

PART ONE

LONELY FOR GOD

In every congregation there will
always be some
with a sense of guilt,
with a sense of emptiness,
with a sense of frustration,
with a sense of injustice,
with a loneliness for God.

After Billy Graham

CHAPTER ONE

THE BRUISING

In the children's playground
you wander aimlessly,
alone.
Afraid of the vibrant, taunting
   group
chanting to its skipping rope.
You play hopscotch,
solitary jacks,
or with whip and top,
alone.
Apparently absorbed,
craving for a friend.

Grown-ups forgot to mention
Jesus would be friendly.

The Isolate
Jenny Cooke, 1975

JENNIFER GRADUALLY WOKE up and became aware that she was gazing at the curtains. She reached for her book, determined to snuggle for the last few minutes into the feather mattress, before Daddy started shouting, 'Get up!' and Mummy asked about her special shoes.

As her hands lingered over her book cover, she gazed at the curtains again. Something was strange...but already she was deep into *The Famous Five*, away at the cove, shutting herself off from that corner of her mind that had remembered today was games at school.

Then her gaze went back to the curtains. Of course! She bounded out of bed and stuck her head between the curtains. It had snowed. The fields, the lane, the trees, everywhere was white. Everywhere looked different. Perhaps, then, today would be different and there'd be no games. She stared out of the window. Her eyebrows puckered and she turned slowly back to her bed. Already Daddy was coming down the landing and she hadn't finished her chapter yet. She shivered and reached for her vest. Perhaps, just perhaps, today would be different. She sighed and fumbled over her liberty bodice. There was a chance, after all. A very small chance. But the leaden weight that always seemed to lodge on her chest on weekdays, was settling there as usual.

After breakfast she set off to trudge the two miles to school, her hands pushed deep in her pockets, her wellingtons squelching in the snow. She could see the long, wriggly cycle track her dad had made as he'd wobbled down the lane to work. She turned and waved to her mother who was framed in the doorway. Then her mum went back into the house and Jennifer was on her own.

She stood for a moment and gazed at the hawthorn hedge. It was a tangle of black thorns, crusted with snow. She half closed her eyes and the tree shone in the sunlight like a fairy's diamond palace. Oh, it's pretty, she thought. Pretty. And a smile curved around her cheeks.

But her satchel weighed heavily on her shoulders and she knew she mustn't linger. Mr Smart didn't like children being late for Prayers. So she set her face in the direction of the school and trudged on. She pushed back her hair under her hat and felt the kirby grip. I wish I had curly hair, she thought, and scragged her hair back even further behind her ears.

She came round the corner and suddenly stopped. She stared blankly in front of her. Everything was white. And the lane had gone. She looked round and nothing but the immensity of whiteness and snowiness met her eyes. But where was the lane? She took a step back and looked again. There was Mrs Rice's cottage. And on the other side stood Mrs Long's, squat and grey. But where was the lane that always wound between them?

Jennifer blinked and then lurched forwards. Her wellingtons sank in the snow and she felt an icy trickle on her socks. As she got closer to the whiteness she suddenly realized what it was. It was a wall of snow. The snow must have filled up the lane during the night and made a wall from one side to the other, almost joining the two cottages. She laboured up to the wall, each step slower than the last.

Finally she got there and looked up at the snow wall. It was bigger than she was. She turned round and stared behind her. No one was about. Only her own line of footprints marched stolidly up to the wall. She was quite alone. She frowned and then bit her lip. She turned to face the wall, plonked her right foot into the bottom of it and tried to haul herself up. But her other foot slipped and she staggered back. She tried again. This time she got half way up, but thumped backwards again into the snow. Again she tried. Again she fell.

'Mum,' she whimpered. Bur her mother couldn't come. Jennifer's throat tightened and her eyes pricked. Her face went red and her fists clenched. She picked herself up and half strode, half staggered to the part of the wall nearest Mrs Rice's cottage. She stuck her chin out and hurled herself at the wall. Somehow, she clawed at the snow and clambered upwards; her wellingtons filled with snow, her face smarted and her mittens became caked with cold, but somehow she got to the top and rolled herself over the other side.

She picked herself up, shook the snow out of her eyes and trundled on down the lane. Her feet were cold but her face was one big grin. She tried to do a hop and a skip and a jump, then lurched forward and clasped her hands together. She'd done it! She'd climbed a wall, no, a mountain of snow. She, who was always picked last for the team games at school, had climbed a mountain of snow. And her cheeks shone.

Her grin lasted nearly all the way to school. But as she drew nearer her pace slackened, until she nearly stopped. She dragged her feet up to the school railings and stood and stared at the playground beyond. Everywhere children were playing, shouting and laughing. Everywhere they played in gangs. Jennifer's shoulders drew into a hunch, her hands drooped into her pockets and her expression went quite dead, as if blinds were suddenly drawn down. She hovered near the wall, drew in her breath and then made her feet march through the gate.

It was as if a space cleared itself around her. She crept along by the wall, hoping to make the shelter of the school door, hoping no one would notice her and try to grab her hat.

This time she made the doorway safely. She leaned against the stones and waited. And watched the children playing. She stood as stiff as a ramrod, her face set into solid lines. Nothing given away. Then she lifted her chin ever so slightly. Bet none of *them* climbed a mountain of snow to get to school, she thought, and for a moment her eyes lightened.

A gang of girls from 3B suddenly rushed towards her, yelling 'Gotcha!' and 'Tig!' Jennifer stood up very straight and her cheeks went pink. They were going to ask her to play with them. Yes they were! She took a step or two forward. The girls charged all around her, laughing and tugging at each other. For a moment she was at the centre of a whirlpool of legs and arms. Then, just as suddenly, they were gone.

She stayed as if frozen to the wall. Something, something

stopped her from running in amongst them and slapping them on their backs and giggling over a daft joke. Something seemed to be frozen inside her, making everything stiff. But underneath that frost beat a heart that longed to join in.

She gazed after them and then, ever so slowly, pulled her satchel off her back. She unfastened it and let her hands linger over her library books. For a few seconds she forgot she stood alone, with her back against the old school wall. She looked at the bright covers, the stories of popular girls who won all the prizes at the Pony Club, and she smiled. She counted her books, first from left to right. And then from right to left. She checked that all her pencils and crayons were there. And then, when there was nothing left to check, or re-check, she slowly, ever so slowly, did up the buckles again.

Later on in the classroom, Jennifer slouched in her seat and gazed blankly out of the steamy windows. She pretended to be getting on with her Comprehension in case Mr Smart noticed her, but really she'd finished it long ago. She chewed her pencil and stared at her exercise book, neatly pencil written. She knew all her answers were right and so, in case the others called her swot, she rubbed out one or two of the correct answers and wrote in wrong ones instead.

Suddenly a chair creaked and scraped. She looked up. Michael Fish had put his hand up. He always sat in the middle of a clutch of grubby boys and he usually spent his days making paper darts and giggling. His clothes were lank and he smelled of fish. Jennifer wrinkled her nose. What would Old Smartie say now? Michael Fish never asked questions.

'Sir,' called Michael Fish. The whole class stopped writing and leaned back in their chairs, glad of any excuse to stop, while their pencils went spattering over the floor.

'Sir!'

Mr Smart dragged his eyes from a book and began to drum his fingers on his desk. 'I don't want to hear anything at the moment, Michael. Have you finished your work?'

'Er, no. But....'

'Well get on then!'

'But, Sir!'

Mr Smart sighed heavily. 'Well, boy, what is it?'

'Please, Sir, er, Sir....'

Mr Smart adjusted his glasses on his face. 'Get on with it, boy!'

There was a long silence and then MIchael burst out, 'Please, Sir, who made God?'

An even longer silence met his question, a silence so complete in that chalk-filled classroom that it seemed as if time itself had stopped. Mr Smart's fingers were still now. Jennifer leaned forward and her hand went to her mouth. Her face was alight with wonder. What a question! Who *had* made God? In that silence she suddenly realized it was the only question she'd ever really be interested in, or really wanted to know the answer to. All the rows and rows of boring comprehension answers she'd done in that classroom were as nothing to this. She leaned forward, eager and ready.

Mr Smart stirred. Jennifer looked at him quickly and her face was laughing. He'd know. She was sure of that. He always knew everything. He cleared his throat, 'Well, I, er, I....'

She waited. She looked at Michael Fish. He had his head cocked on one side, leaning on his hand and his eyes were bright. He really wants to know, she thought surprised. He wants to know as much as I do.

She shifted in her chair. Why wasn't Old Smartie yelling out the answer like he usually did? Then the teacher spoke and his eyes were fixed to his desk lid. 'I'm sorry, Michael. No one, er, knows the answer to that. He must have, er, made himself.'

The class tittered and Michael Fish went red and grinned foolishly. Jennifer stared at her teacher and her face creased with puzzlement. Mr Smart didn't *know*. She frowned. All of a sudden the day had gone flat. Michael Fish was chucking darts again. If only she knew...but there was the bell for playtime. And the question was left unanswered, to be put away with the jumble of books into her desk.

She hung back, the last to leave the classroom. She spun out the moments in the cloakroom, putting on her hat and coat and wellingtons in slow motion. But at last she had to go into the playground. She knew that if she sidled along by the railings to the 'lavs' the longest way round, a few more minutes would be used up. But they smelled and all too soon she was back into the playground again. She wandered around near the porch until she saw the teacher coming round the corner, and then pretended to be busy scrabbling in the snow. At last the teacher tolled the handbell and there was a mad dash for the lines. As she stood in her line, Jennifer's back went a bit straighter. Only two more lessons and then home-time. Toast and celery by the fire and if Daddy was in a good mood, she'd be able to stay up till half past seven and listen to *The Barlows of Beddington* on the wireless. Mummy always wanted to hear about her marks and her lessons and perhaps she'd know who made God. So with a lightening of her step, she trotted into her classroom.

CHAPTER TWO

THE CRUSHING

Crushed by parents' quarrels
you retreat into exams.
You sit at desk
alone;
hiding rejection with books,
comforted by penny sweets.
Over the dreary years
misery settles like heavy clay
into your subsoil;
loneliness
your constant, apathetic friend.

Grown-ups forgot to mention
Jesus would be friendly.

The Isolate
Jenny Cooke, 1975

JENNIFER ROUNDED THE cinder path to their house and shot up the drive, taking the back steps two at a time, and half fell into the scullery.

'Mum!' she yelled.

'Hello, dear.'

'What's for pudding?'

'Treacle sponge.'

Like a door slamming on all the darkness, Jennifer forgot the school and the beastly team games, the wall of snow and the wind moaning in the tree branches. At home she was safe. She could slouch and eat toffees and read books. Mummy was there. Good, kind mummy.

And even if Daddy was cross when he came in, he'd bounce her and Lizzie on the beds after tea. Then he'd stump off upstairs to the attic, and a few minutes later there'd be a mysterious sound of hammering. She and Lizzie weren't allowed to go up there.

'Do as you're told!' shouted Daddy one evening as they tried creeping up the second flight of stairs in the darkness. Then, 'Rotten kids sniffing round!' But how strange and wonderful on that haloed Christmas morning. Jennifer woke up and felt a weight and rustle at the end of her bed. Strange that Father Christmas hadn't left them much. And then, wonderful! Downstairs in the drawing-room, there, in the corner, was a little house, big enough to stand up inside, with curtains and windows. And a door, just wide enough for her to go through. Daddy was right behind her, joking and asking how on earth the old gentleman had got it down the chimney. Lizzie was squeaking and squealing in another corner. There, in exactly the same pinks and blues as Jennifer's house, was a little shop for her sister. Blue shelves and jars full of dolly mixtures and some scales and grease-proof paper bags.

'Oh,' said Jennifer and clasped her hands together. 'Oh, it's lovely. Lovely.'

Then Aunty Mary and Uncle Leslie came for Christmas lunch and gave both the girls new, electric-blue party dresses. Aunty Mary kissed and hugged them and all the lights on the Christmas tree were reflected in the golden balls that hung from a necklace that she wore.

All too soon Christmas was over. Jennifer had to go back to school. Then Mummy began to get pains in her tummy and had to go to hospital for an operation. Daddy got more and more cross and said that if they were naughty he'd use the strap.

One day after Mummy had come home from hospital and was resting, Jennifer said, 'Why's Daddy cross all the time?'

'He's tired, dear.'

Jennifer stared at her hands. But Daddy was always tired, always angry, always shouting, never smiling. For as long as she could remember he had been angry with her and Lizzie, so that they crept round the house, hoping he wouldn't notice them, keeping very still and quiet when he came into the room. She looked up. There in the corner was the Wendy House with its pretty wall paper and hand-made curtains and even a hand-painted picture hanging on the wall. She frowned and bit her nails. She didn't understand. She didn't understand at all. All she knew was that her father shouted and shouted about their toys scattered on the floor and about how she and Lizzie were stupid children, until she felt exhausted and whipped by that voice.

Then another memory edged into her mind. It had been a winter night and she woke up with ear-ache, sobbing and moaning and rocking her head in her hands. It was Daddy she remembered, who came and held her in his arms and pressed his hands to her ears to make her pain go away and who tied on the fur hood her mother had made to keep her ears warm.

She looked over to her mother. 'Mum, why's Dad tired all the time?'

Her mother sighed. 'He has to ride a long way to work and back on his bicycle. It's a long way to Dewsbury. And it's uphill. He's dead beat when he gets in.'

'Oh.' Jennifer's brow puckered. She didn't know grown-ups got dead beat. Mummy sat very still in her armchair and then said, 'Give Elizabeth her bread and dripping, will you?' Sprinkle a little bit of salt on it for her.'

Jennifer looked at her mother. Her voice had gone very quiet and her face looked white. Jennifer picked up the plate and passed it to her sister. She knocked the salt over and her mummy sighed again and said nothing. Jennifer scowled. She was always the one who knocked things over. Children called her 'Fatty' at school. She glared at Lizzie, pretty, dainty Lizzie with her golden, curly hair, and stumped across the kitchen to the window.

It was some time later that grown-ups and teachers began talking about the Eleven-Plus. Old Smartie chuntered on about it nearly every day. Then her dad started. 'I've no money to give you, so you'd better use your brains and pass the Eleven-Plus. That's the only way you'll ever get on in this world, my girl. By using your brains.'

She opened her mouth and then closed it again. There was nothing she could say.

One Saturday morning her Mum dressed her up in her Sunday clothes. Jennifer pulled off the green, woolly hat and stuffed it into her pocket. 'What do I have to wear these for?'

'You and Daddy are going to church,' said Mummy.

'But it's Saturday! Church is boring!'

'You're going.'

Daddy held her hand firmly as they walked there. She felt shy as she trotted along beside him. She couldn't remember the two of them ever going anywhere together before.

'Dad,' she said, 'what we going to church for?'

'Well,' said her father and cleared his throat, 'well, er, I want to ask God to bless you in the Eleven-Plus.'

'Oh,' she said, trying to sound as if she understood this strange, grown-up behaviour.

When they got to the church it was dark inside. The vicar was waiting by the altar and candles were glimmering near him. He was wearing a golden cloak with embroidery on it. She shrank next to her father and he held her hand tightly. The vicar smiled but behind his eyes he seemed tired, as if his thoughts were elsewhere. He beckoned them forward and motioned them to kneel together at the altar rail. She stared at the carpet. It was green. The vicar began to pray and then put his hands on her head. She stayed, stock still, head bent, face red.

'Oh God, please bless Jennifer in her Eleven-Plus exam.'

She was puzzled. She had never thought of her name and God's name all in one sentence before. Then it was over. And she and her Dad escaped into the dusty lanes and hedgerows, all lacy with weeds and flowers.

One morning, months later, she was called out of Prayers and sent to the headmaster's study. Five other children crowded in along with her. She guessed why she had been called and her step quickened. Old Rolypoly adjusted his spectacles and beamed at them. 'You have all done extremely well,' he said. 'You have all passed the Eleven-Plus.' Jennifer felt her face swelling with pride. Old Rolypoly clapped his hand on her shoulder. 'And you have done very well indeed, my girl. Only ten years old and you have passed the Eleven-Plus.'

Her pride lasted until she sat down again in the classroom. Then she bit her nails. What about all the others? The rows and rows of chairs in 4A, each one with a child who hadn't passed. There had been no one at all from 4B in Rolypoly's study either. She looked at their faces: set, stolid, no smiles. She glanced at the few girls who had finally let her hang around on the edge of their group in the playground. They'd let her hold the rope, while they skipped to the skipping rhymes. They wouldn't look at her now, but stared at their desks. And something like a stone settled into her heart. Only one other girl in the whole school, Margaret Bolshaw, would be going along to the Grammar School with her. She looked at Margaret who looked back with an uncertain smile. Jennifer clenched her fist round her pencil. Why, oh why, did she have to be clever? She rammed her pencil hard on to the desk lid. The point broke and the pencil fell, spoiled, to the floor.

Like all the other buildings in the town, the Grammar School was black with soot. Day in and day out Jennifer stumped past its black gates. As the days lengthened into weeks, months and years she got used to shouldering her heavy satchel, she got used to the long, uphill walk home, the bitter winters and their dark old house at the top of the hill.

Her parents watched her change from a plump, little girl full of noise and bounce who was always squabbling with her sister, to a taller, thinner girl; a girl whose fingers were always ink-stained, whose homework was blotched and whose school books were dog-eared. Her marks slumped into the low grades. She never brought home friends. And her face got quieter and more shuttered as if no emotion lurked there.

When her mother unfurled the school photograph one afternoon she saw that someone had neatly scribbled out one of the faces and made it into a black square. When she asked Jennifer why she had done this, Jennifer merely hung her head and turned away.

'You naughty girl! Your father would have been proud of seeing you on the photograph!'

But Jennifer would not turn round.

Her mother looked at her, with her flat, silk bob of golden hair and over-sturdy legs, and ached for her. Where were Jennifer's friends? Why didn't she giggle and laugh like other girls? There were times when Jennifer was happy, her mother knew that. Like when she ran off to feed apple cores to her friend, Prince, who whinneyed and frisked when he saw her coming down the lane; or when she tumbled into the kitchen with an armful of bluebells picked from the fields near the Open-Cast mine. Or when she read. And read. And read book after book from the Public Library. But as her mother now finally realized, there were no friends. She watched as Jennifer gazed out of the window at the red May tree that grew at the bottom of the garden, gazing and gazing, eyes lit up as if with wonder. Her satchel was slung in one corner, her school hat trampled under a chair and her cardigan buttoned up on the wrong holes. Her mother's lips set into a firm line. Something was going to be done. And with a toss of her head she went into the scullery to peel potatoes.

Jennifer saw her mother at the sink. She knew she ought to go and help but somehow she stayed rooted to the chair. She turned her head away and stared unseeingly out of the window. The school photograph lay in a white roll on the table and she put her hand out to touch it, then drew it away again. Why had she blacked out her own face? She stared blankly at the table. She simply didn't know. But part of her said, yes you do know. You're fat and ugly and have got straight hair and no friends and no one likes you and no one ever, ever, ever plays with you at break and Daddy's always, always cross and Mummy's been ill and the work's boring at school and you're no good at games... she drew her face into set lines, her shoulders hunched and her chin raised slightly. She'd have to go back to school tomorrow. So there was no point in thinking about it now. Best just to see if there were a few sweets in the cupboard and a nice pony book from the library and blow school.

But as she went to search for the sweets the rolled-up photograph drew her eyes again. She remembered the tiny blacked-out face in the middle row and it was as if that person didn't exist. *But I am me,* she thought suddenly and the fierceness of the thought made her start up from her chair and knock her book from the edge of the table. So why did she feel heavy and awkward with other girls, she asked herself yet again. She simply didn't know. She didn't understand at all.

There was a noise of shouting and then more shouting and a crashing against the dining-room door. Jennifer shrank against the wall and waited. She and Lizzie must have left their toys out again. She stayed still but the shouting stopped after a few moments. She let her breath out in a gasp and her hands reached to find the bag of cheap boiled sweets in the cupboard. She went and sat down again with the white paper bag crushed in her fist. It wasn't just the shouting at home that lashed her mind. There was other and worse shouting at school. At least at home she knew Daddy liked playing with them and the very next week he had promised to take them to Dewsbury Feast. But at school it was so much worse. She shuddered suddenly and the paper bag remained unopened.

She remembered the Scripture teacher, her voice whip-lashing the room, her gaze like ice. 'Jennifer Appleby *never* addresses me properly! Does she? Does she?'

And her own face smarting and her knuckles white as she gazed like a rabbit in a trap at the set face of the teacher. Her mind was a blank. What did the teacher want? What did she want her to say? Another girl told her later. 'You forgot to say, "Yes, Miss Mannering." You forgot to use her name.'

Then there had been the Domestic Science teacher whose face got more and more sour as the term went on, until one day she snatched up Jennifer's apron with its clumsy stitching and soiled edges and threw it, crumpled, to the floor. Her voice was like acid in the room and all the other girls stopped their work and looked up and stared at Jennifer and her burning face. Then they all turned away and got on with their work and when the lesson was over she pushed the damp apron into her satchel and slowly, ever so slowly, trudged out into the playground, alone as usual.

The worst thing of all had been when an older girl, Jane Blake, with a greasy face, forced her to put salt into a prefect's glass of water; then there'd been the prefect shouting and she terrified and lying that she hadn't done it. The weight of that lie and the fear of Jane Blake scarred her mind. The whole class found out and ganged up on her, and one girl got her in front of all the others and demanded to know why she hadn't told the truth. And when she opened her mouth to try and explain, somehow the only thing that came out was the lie again. So after that they all left her severely alone. And she knew that no one would stand up for her against Jane Blake.

Jennifer pulled a sweet out of the bag. She sucked hard at her favourite colour, an orange fruit drop. Deliberately she pushed all the memories away for a while and leaned back in the chair and found her book. At least now there was some peace. But this time the memories stayed with her all through the chapter.

Months later, when they were on holiday at St Ives, her father called her to him one morning. 'Jennifer, we've got some news.'

She looked at him and waited.

'We're leaving Yorkshire.'

Her mouth fell open.

He stared at her, as if trying to find words.

She stared back, hardly knowing what to think.

He said, 'You'll not be going back to that school!'

'But...' she began.

'We're going to live in Macclesfield. I've transferred my job.' There was a pause. 'It's a new start. For all of us.'

An incredulous delight sprang through her. Words rushed into her mouth, but she didn't know how to say them.

There was a silence.

'You'll be happier at the new school,' he said.

She nodded. 'Yes, Dad.'

There was another pause.

'Off you go to play then.'

'Yes, Dad.'

After breakfast she ran to the beach and hugged the news to herself. It spread with a warmth all over her body. She was never going to have to go back to that school again! Never walk round that interminable playground again. Never sit on her own again. She clenched her fists and lifted her chin ever so slightly. She was going to make friends at the new school. She knew she would. She sat on, while the full, sweet meaning dawned on her. The sun warmed her face and a smile curved her cheeks. She leaned back on the sand and watched the sea.

Two memories came back to her. There had only been twice in those two long, long years when she remembered actually enjoying a lesson. Once when she read a book by a man with a strange name and she forgot everything in the absorption of reading about him as a young and lonely boy. She turned back to the cover of the book and tried to memorize his name: it was Siegfried Sassoon. But then Miss Taylor jerked in and took the books away and made them do a daft essay on Highwaymen and she only got 'B Minus' for her mark.

The other time was when Miss Mannering was away and Miss Taylor took them for Scripture. She read out a passage about the beginning of the world. Jennifer remembered gradually tuning in to that lesson, her slouch giving way to alert shoulders as she leant forward on the edge of her chair.

'I don't believe there is a God,' said Miss Taylor. Her face was old-looking, but she wore young clothes. Her lipstick was a gash of red and her hair jagged, angrily sticking out from her face. 'I don't believe in a God. But it's strange how in Genesis the seven days, or epochs, of creation seem to largely parallel the order in which scientists think evolution took place....'

Jennifer sat up, her face alive with questions. She longed to know, to listen, to hear about how the world was made. She began to raise her hand. Then the bell went and the moment was lost. The following week Miss Mannering was back, crushing any interest in creation by fear of the whiplash voice.

Jennifer got up off the sand and slowly walked back to the rented holiday cottage. Well, now she was never going to have to hear that voice again, nor go back to that school. It was over. Her back was very straight. She was going to find a friend in Macclesfield. That was definite. She hesitated by the wall and then grinned. She'd get her mum to cut her hair into a fringe, instead of scragging it back with kirby grips and she'd buy some setting lotion from the chemist and make curls. Yes. And she'd not call herself Jennifer any more. No, from now on she was going to be called Jenny. It would be a new name for a new person, and she skipped through the cottage doorway.

But the shadow of the past was to remain.

CHAPTER THREE

THE DARK PEARL

I thought to follow Christ would
mean
a dull routine of Sunday best,
unperceptive talk about the status
quo,
a loss of stature and a thrust of
tracts,
unworthy prayer, unlovely clothes:
a safe reduction to the middle
way…

Jenny Cooke, 1977

On her first morning at Macclesfield High School Jenny walked into the classroom after the headmistress. She fixed her eyes on that steely, upright back, straight as a ramrod beneath tight Paisley silk. There was a pause as the form teacher took in the details about the new girl.

Jenny clenched her hands in her blazer pockets. Then, slowly, she raised her head and turned to face the class. She put her face into a smile and held it. Then her eyes fell and her hands clenched tighter than ever. No one smiled. No one moved. And no one frowned.

She heard nothing of that first lesson, glad to be left alone at a side desk. After a while the familiar bell jangled and there was a crash of desk lids. Girls surged towards the door. Jenny watched their backs and the old, leaden feeling began to settle round her heart. No, she thought. No! I will make friends. She lifted her chin and smiled at no one in particular.

All at once a girl smiled back. She came up and held out her hand. 'Hiya,' she said.

'Hiya,' said Jenny, her heart thumping.

'You new?'

'Yep.'

'Want to come out for break?'

'Oh yes, please.'

Jenny followed her. The girl grinned and took off her glasses. Then she thrust her hand into her tunic pocket and drew out a bar of chocolate, 'Like a piece?'

'Thank you.'

The girl put her glasses back on and broke the chocolate in half. 'My name's Christine Turnock. What's yours?'

'Jenny Appleby.'

'Well come on then. I'll show you the grounds.'

And later that afternoon as Jenny half ran home to their new house on the bright, new housing estate, everything about the town seemed to glow, from the mellow brick of the High School, to the new house, glossy with white paint and full of sunshine.

Friday evening was the night for the parish church Youth Club. Jenny stood in a cluster with the other girls at one end of the seedy church hall. They gazed across the expanse of wooden floorboards to the gang of boys hunched round the record player at the other end. The voices of Cliff Richard and Tommy Steele were rocking and rolling round the room and soon toes and heels were tapping. Eventually the girls partnered each other in the twist and the jive.

Occasionally Jenny caught the eye of one of the boys and then he asked her to dance. Sometimes Barbara Kaye brought her a grubby envelope or a garbled message. 'Sid wants to go out with you.' 'Eric wants to take you to the Pictures.' But there was never any question of her being allowed to go. Her dad was far too strict. 'You're not going out with any boys till you're sixteen!'

Silence.

'No, Dad.'

It was fun all the same. There was always one boy or other who made her cheeks burn and her heart do a sudden lurch, even if all she saw was his back view. And there'd always be another boy she was anxious to avoid, even if he followed her or waited with bitten nails outside her school.

Then one evening the curate came along to the Youth Club and asked if anyone wanted to sign up for the coach trip to hear Billy Graham. Everyone seemed to be signing so she signed up as well.

'Who's Billy Graham?' she asked her parents when she got home. Her mother stared blankly but her dad said, 'You're not going to hear that religious nut are you!'

She put her chin up. 'What if I am?'

'Well don't come back shouting "Jesus! Jesus!" will you!' And he stumped off, chuckling to himself.

She sighed. Dratted parents! Always one step ahead.

The night of the meeting came. Their Youth Club took up three rows of seats in the Manchester stadium. The girls who had boyfriends sat next to them and held hands. Jenny sat in with a group of girls who weren't 'going steady'. She glanced round, saw Eric, and turned quickly away. Since her dad had said she couldn't go to the pictures with him, he seemed to have lost interest in her. Still, at least he wasn't sitting with another girl.

The meeting began. There was a great singing of hymns. There were massed choirs, flowers near the rostrum and the powerful voice of Billy Graham ringing round the auditorium. Then more singing, swelling to the roof. Suddenly the feel of the meeting changed. People were being asked to decide, to make up their minds, to take this opportunity. With a sense of panic Jenny saw different boys and girls standing up in their seats. People were walking down the aisle to the rostrum. But what did it mean? Why were they doing it? She frowned and bit her lip. She half got up and then sat down. All at once she saw Eric pushing his way forward. That did it. She jumped to her feet and followed him, then lost him in the crush. A kindly lady helped her to a seat and tried to talk to her. Jenny kept shaking her head, 'I don't know why I came down...I just....' She twisted her head round but Eric wasn't there.

The kindly lady seemed to sense her hesitation, 'You're young yet, dear. Wait till you're older. But if you give me your name and address may we send you some literature?'

'Er, yes please.'

Slowly Jenny made her way back to her seat. She sat in silence. There was nothing to say. Nothing to say either on the coach going home. Nothing, as the driver dimmed the lights and all the 'steadies' snogged and petted in the semi-darkness, while she sat bolt upright on her seat. She stared unseeing out of the window. Even the awareness of Eric sitting with his arm round Stella Mace didn't seem to matter much now.

The question went round and round in her mind. Why had she gone forward? She knew the answer to that really and despised herself for it. Yet there had been something about the way Billy Graham had said the name of Jesus. It echoed in her mind. People had surged forward, beckoned into the space at the front: a space they filled with the name. Before, she had always associated that name with a figure imprisoned in a stained glass window. Or a face looking white and saintly in her Grandmother's illustrated children's Bible. Jenny's lips clamped together. She wasn't sure she liked this name. She wasn't sure at all.

Later, when the literature arrived through the post, Jenny piled it up neatly on her bookcase. At first she tried to read it. But there were so many other things to do. 'Read this. Learn that. Help at church.' She shrank away from it, from this name that seemed to call to her in the darkness of her room. She knew it wasn't any use anyway. Even when she did read the Bible the language seemed meaningless and old-fashioned. It wasn't like other books.

A lot of girls in her form at school were thrilled to bits with Billy Graham. A group began to meet in different girls' houses.

'We're studying the Bible,' said Karen one day to Jenny. 'Want to come?'

There was a pause, 'Oh, er, yes. Thank you.' After all, over half the class went. She didn't want to be left out.

At the weekly meetings she sat stiffly on a chair, while the others laughed and chatted over orange squash. Then they pulled out their Bibles and a hush fell in those dark rooms, stuffed with too many plush seats and old china. They pored over long, long Authorized Version sentences as Jenny pressed her hands together and tried to stifle that leaden feeling. She didn't understand. Not at all.

Once the leader asked a question in a reverent voice, and in the awkward over-long silence that followed Jenny gazed fixedly at the floor. At last she raised her head and caught the leader's eye. Surely someone could see the answer to a simple question like that. It was easy. It was... but she shrugged and sat on in a pool of silence. There was something horribly familiar about sitting there on the upright chair, with her back against the wall and nobody talking to her. Her mind shut off like a shutter, cutting her off from the memory of what it was. At the end, there seemed to be a space around her as the others laughed and chattered and made further arrangements to meet and somehow never asked her till the pause after the end, when they had all finished making plans.

The 'O' Levels came and went and like most girls in her form Jenny passed them all. School after the fifth form stopped being a chore. The sixth form was different. She loved it. She loved the dreamy afternoons in the art room and the pungent smell of geraniums for the Still Life. She loved the pictures of Old Masters on the school walls and gazed, spellbound, at Corot's dish of apples glowing near the science lab. The elderly art teacher, Miss Cartwright, had hands that fumbled with eagerness as she opened paint tins or found books and pamphlets about modern art. She would pile them up in a jumble on the desk and say, 'Look at that! Look! Look!' And Jenny looked and saw the brilliant colours and rash shapes of Picasso, Mondrian and Cézanne.

She loved the meticulous Geography lessons and the hilarious French lessons but most of all she loved the English lessons and the crackle of excitement in the air as her teacher, Miss Dent, swooped into *King Lear* and the words carved the air.

Her mind took the challenge and began to chart its own course. Somewhere in the middle of absorbing all the crash and clash of modern art; somehow, in the discovery of modern writers like Jean-Paul Sartre and Ionesco and their bleak prose, with no beginnings and no endings but only middles; somehow, in the midst of all the sixth-form parties and the going steady with the Youth Club leader; somehow, she lost her little faith.

She didn't even know she'd lost it until one day in the geography room. Miss Bluck was delayed and Jenny picked up a book off the shelf and began reading idly from the middle. 'There can be no God,' she read. 'Such an idea is foolish to the modern mind.... The world evolved to its present state over millions of years.... The six days of creation are an absurdity...our future is in our own hands.'

She dropped the book to the desk. The other three girls looked round. She leaned back in her chair until it was at a dangerous angle and said, 'You'll never guess what!'

'What now?'

'I don't believe in God any more!' And she began to laugh.

'It's stupid. Unintelligent.' She sat and waited for Karen to argue. She remembered the Karen of the Bible Study meetings, with her earnest testimony and hushed voice. She stared at Karen's back, waited, and then repeated, 'There's no God!' Karen's back leaned further over her books, her shoulders round with strain, her pen flying across the page.

'No God,' said Jenny, louder than ever.

But there was silence.

Why didn't Karen shout back and argue? Jenny wanted to argue, to disagree, to pull down the other side. But still Karen's shoulders hunched. Jenny's chair scraped and crashed back into position again. She felt her face glow with victory. Karen was scared. And another girl was eagerly reading the atheistic book.

'I'm an existentialist,' Jenny boasted to her dad that evening. She patted her hair. 'You know, the Theatre of the Absurd and all that.'

'Hummmph,' he said and paused. 'Get on with your homework.'

When Sunday came she trailed to church with the family as usual. The service passed over her head. Her mind was too full of going up to Leeds University in the autumn, of leaving home. 'The world's your oyster,' said Uncle Leslie each time she saw him.

At the communion rail she took the cup and stared into the depths of red wine. The candle glimmer was reflected there and suddenly her eyes pricked. As she drank, she thought, 'How sad, how terrible. Jesus was a good man.' But there was nothing behind him. Nothing but... nothing. Nothing in the space to which people had flocked that night when they heard Billy Graham preach the name. Nothing beyond the cup, but the cup. For the first time a flicker of fear passed over her. If nothing was there, then why was she...? She pushed away the question and went firmly back to her seat. She was going to find the pearl in the oyster, even if it was a dark one.

CHAPTER FOUR

THE STORM WITHIN

I searched for years to find if God
were there,
pacing the streets of the mind, with
Nothing
as my companion in the night....

The Search
Jenny Cooke, 1977

The day came when Jenny staggered downstairs with the last bulging package and dumped it in the hall. Her dad glared at all the luggage. 'How on earth am I going to get all that lot in?'

But at last it was all stowed away and Jenny climbed into the front seat. Her mum kissed her and then went and stood bravely by the front door, waving and saying, 'Take care, dear, and don't get cold, and don't stay up too late!'

'Well,' said her dad, 'it's time for off. No use hanging about!'

Jenny craned round to get a last view of her mum before the car shot round the corner, waved, and then she was gone. Jenny settled back in her seat. The journey had begun.

The car climbed over the bleak moorlands and Pennine hills back to Yorkshire. Up and up they went until, at last, they were at the highest point of the road.

'You can see Leeds from here,' said her dad.

She looked and saw a vast sprawl far away and factory smoke in the air and her heart gave a jump and her eyes sparkled. She didn't reply but clasped her hands tightly round her knees. Her heart fluttered with excitement. She was going to be on her own!

Suddenly she bit her lip. She remembered the day of her interview at the University. She met the tutor of Arts' Studies, a massive woman who sat with her back to the window and blocked out the light. She said quite impassively, 'Miss Appleby, I see you come from Yorkshire originally. And now you're wanting to come back and study here. Does that mean you were so happy here you can't wait to come back?'

Jenny stared at the tutor and finally stammered out, 'Er, well, er, yes I suppose it was the course here that I wanted to study,' while her mind froze with the memory of herself as a young child, alone, in that hateful playground. Happy here? The tutor sized her up, waited, and then snapped shut her file. 'We can offer you a place,' she said.

Jenny ran down the steps to her dad who was waiting in the car, 'I've got a place! I've got a place if I get the right 'A' Levels!' Her eyes were very bright and her cheeks shone. She *was* going to be happy in Yorkshire this time.

Now as Leeds got nearer she lifted her chin high and slammed the lid down hard on her memories. Soon the car was twisting up the drive to Weetwood Hall of Residence, past late, brilliant dahlias, up to the Jacobean porch. They found her room. And then came the last moment. Her dad pushed his flat cap back on his head. 'Goodbye, love. Good luck.'

'Bye, Dad.'

They stood looking at each other for a moment and then she pecked him on the cheek and he patted her on the arm, turned, and stumped off. She watched him go, hardly aware of the stamina he'd need to do the long Pennine haul for the second time in one day.

She began to unpack her clothes from the second-hand trunk. At the bottom lay her books. She took them out, and there, half hidden under a tome on the Anglo-Saxons was the old Bible her Grandmother had once given her. She hesitated over it and finally stuffed it at one end of the bookshelf where it couldn't be seen easily.

One morning Jenny staggered down for breakfast at the last minute. She poured out some coffee to help stifle her yawns and found a quiet corner by the window. She sat for a few minutes staring blankly out on to the lawns, while her fingers played idly with a letter half tucked into her jeans pocket. She pulled out the creased envelope and a smile hovered round her face as she reread it.

'Thank you for your last letter,' her mother had written. 'We knew it was from you, even though it finished mid-sentence and was unsigned!'

Jenny giggled. It was just like her to have forgotten to sign a letter. She sipped some coffee and settled down to read more. As she did so she became oblivious to all the chit-chat around her. At last she smoothed out the letter again and then folded it neatly and put it back into her pocket. But her mother's words were insistent. 'Have you ever thought of becoming a writer?' she wrote. 'Your great-grandfather was an editor on *The Hull Daily Mail* for years. Your father and I think you have got it in you to become a writer. You take after great-grandfather. And we love reading your letters....'

Jenny took the letter out of her pocket once more and stared at it. There had been a time at school in the fifth year, when she had got so immersed in reading poems up by the school canal, that she'd nearly missed a lesson. But as for writing, well, that was something she'd never thought about. She shook her head thoughtfully. She left the dining-room and went slowly up the stairs to her room. Then she stuffed the letter in a drawer and let her mother's words slip to the back of her mind.

One day some weeks later Jenny was sitting reading in her room when she heard voices outside. Jane's laugh floated up the stairs and Jenny put her book down. No doubt it was Jane coming back early with her latest boyfriend, 'The Magnificent Michael' as they had dubbed him. Suddenly Jane burst in, followed by a strange young man. Jenny stared at him. He looked like a young bull with a great shock of black hair and huge shoulders.

Jane said, 'This is Tim. You know, Michael's flat-mate.'

Jenny grinned. Since Michael had come into Jane's life, she had taken to going red when his name was mentioned. Jenny looked over to Tim.

'Hi!' she said.

'Hello,' said Tim.

When he'd gone Jane said, 'Honestly the way he was looking at you, you'd think he'd never seen a girl before!'

'Don't be daft!'

'Honestly.'

Jenny put her nose further into her book. 'What's he do?' she mumbled.

Jane said casually, 'Oh, he only got a First in Pure Maths

and is doing a Ph.D. and will probably become a lecturer or something. Quite a catch really.' Jenny suddenly dropped the book, picked up a cushion and threw it at Jane.

The next evening there was a phone call for Jenny. She ran down the stairs and her cheeks were hot.

'Hello,' she said into the receiver.

There was a silence.

'Hello,' she said, a little louder.

'Er, hello, this is, er, Tim speaking.'

There was another pause.

Then he spoke again. 'I was wondering if you, er, would like to come out for dinner with me on Saturday. Jane and Michael are coming.'

'Oh,' said Jenny and her voice came out all squeaky. 'Er, yes, thank you very much.'

'Saturday then. I'll call for you at eight o'clock.'

'Er, yes.'

'Bye.'

'Bye.' She put the receiver down and stood for a moment in shocked silence. No one like Tim had ever asked her out before.

From that Saturday evening she joined the ranks of those who always had a partner. For everything. She was never alone. Everywhere she went, Tim came too. To the shops, the sandwich-bar, the Art Gallery, to dances. If a day passed without them meeting, he phoned her up.

One Sunday in May she got ready quickly after breakfast and then Tim called for her and they went to the park. She ran on ahead and twirled round under the trees. She half closed her eyes and watched the light cascade through the leaves, in filtered greens. All the trees became a whirl and she was at the dizzy centre, arms outstretched. 'Tim,' she called, 'look at that!' He caught up with her and grabbed her arm.

'Look,' she cried, 'I want to hug it all to me, all that beauty and light, for ever.' She turned to face him. 'Tim, do you know what?'

'What?'

'Constable said that England was the only country that had dark sunlight. Can you imagine that? Light that is dark?'

He frowned and stared at her. 'Come on,' he said, and

pulled her along.

After a while they stopped and leaned over a little bridge, watching the water below. She ran her hands along the stone parapet. 'Feel it,' she said. 'It's warm. It's....' But the words trailed away. She stopped and looked up at him. 'What's the matter?' she said.

'It's you. You go to a place—I don't understand it. I can't follow you into all this poetry...and this Constable.' He shrugged. 'You're not like other girls I've been out with.'

She felt herself go cold. 'What do you mean?'

'You're always on about the beauty of nature and everything.'

'Oh. I see.' But she didn't see. Not at all.

He walked quickly to a seat and she came and sat next to him.

'You see, Jenny, I....'

She waited. Waited for all their togetherness to snap.

He cleared his throat. 'I...I think I love you...and one day I'd like to marry someone like you.'

Jenny sat, hardly daring to breathe. She gazed up at him from under her fringe. 'I feel the same,' she whispered.

They ran back to Weetwood Hall across the fields, hands clasped tightly, while the day seemed to have gone golden all around them. As they crossed the courtyard she suddenly saw the church gang wending their way back up the drive, faces alight and laughing. She clasped Tim's hand even tighter and turned her back on them. She knew now her future was secure.

Her parents were silent when she told them the news. Her mother said, 'You're too young. Only eighteen. And,' there was a pause, 'and I always thought you'd marry a man a lot older than yourself.'

Jenny stared blankly at her mother. 'Don't be ridiculous, Mum. Anyway, Tim is older than me.'

I don't know what your father will say. Look, don't you think you're just in love with the idea of being "in love"?'

Her father's face had gone red. You're not marrying anybody until you're twenty-one!' he shouted.

'But that's ages away!'

'While I'm contributing to your education at the University, you'll do as you're told!'

She turned and ran from the room, banged the door, stormed upstairs, threw herself on her bed and clenched her fists into the pillow. Her face set into heavy lines and her mouth pouted. Why couldn't her dad be in favour with something she wanted to do, for once? But she knew him. He wouldn't change his mind. 'Well I'll show you,' she muttered, and sat on alone up there for the rest of the evening.

But as it turned out the summer holidays were a peaceful time. As the days passed she became aware that she had not missed Tim. He seemed to fade into a smallness in her imagination and not be a part of her any more.

Until she got back to Leeds, that was. Then he was real. Then he was big and powerful, demanding all her time and energy. She found that if she slipped down to the town centre between lectures, she could be alone and quiet. Sometimes she went to the Art Gallery and gazed at the Henry Moore sculptures. Sometimes she wandered round the streets, savouring the people. Once she went into a dark city church that smelled of incense. She watched and waited in her pew but nothing happened.

Always when she got back to the campus he was there, waiting. As the term went on the frown marks on his forehead deepened, as she explained, over and over again, that her father wouldn't let them get engaged till she was older.

One evening they went to a performance of *Waiting For Godot*. Jenny sat completely still, intent on the sparkling dialogue, absorbed by the pathetic figures of the two tramps as they waited; waited and waited endlessly for the Monsieur Godot who never came. At last, when one of the old tramp's trousers fell down, no one in the audience moved, no one tittered, so great was the spell cast by the words and the actors.

On the way home she and Tim walked in silence. Suddenly as she watched the sky she saw a shooting star flash across the dark like a shower of pink fireworks. Then it was gone. She shivered and put her hand in Tim's pocket.

'That's like us,' she said.

'What?'

'Us. That shooting star. We bloom. We're brilliant. Then we're snuffed out. Nothing there. Only the dark.'

'What?'

'I mean we're like those two tramps waiting for Godot. He never came. There's nothing. Nothing and no one to come. Nothing there at all.'

He stopped, shaken by the anguish in her voice. 'Oh, come on,' he said, 'cheer up. You'll feel better in the morning.' But as they walked on he was very quiet.

The darkness of that night did not leave her. It seeped into her heart and slowly, as the second year ticked away, began to undergird all her thinking. She took to tramping the streets, rather than riding on buses, and as she walked to and from the University, or Tim's flat, questions haunted her. 'Why are you alive?' they asked. 'What's the meaning of life? Of your life?' And most insistent of all, 'Is there a God?' And behind it all she found nothing but the dark.

To stop the din of questions in her mind she threw herself into a frenzied social whirl. She went out every night. She organized a Ball at Weetwood Hall. She danced and danced until she was exhausted, but when she finally fell into bed the questions came hammering back. She looked at herself in the mirror one day and as she pushed back her heavy toffee-coloured hair, she realized she felt very old, as if she knew too much for comfort about life. Life seemed two-dimensional. Flat. And behind it all was the dark.

At parties she startled young men in the middle of the dance floor by asking, 'Do you believe in a God?'

'Er…er, I don't know.' And their expressions said, 'And I don't care either.'

And always Tim was watching her, not answering her questions. And his brow grew darker.

Every now and then Tim tried to pin her down. 'You're my girl now and we ought to get married as soon as your father says yes. I want to make plans.'

She tried to put him off. 'I'll decide later. I'll ask Dad next vac. It'll be all right, you'll see.' She refused to have a ring but chose an old-gold chain and locket instead.

One Saturday evening she came back to the Hall earlier

than usual. It was past midnight but she didn't feel sleepy. There was something that had been at the back of her mind all day, something she remembered about trees and dark light. She pulled out a pad of paper and began to hurl words down on the page. The words surged up from her mind and her hands could hardly keep up with her fingers. There was no time. She knew she had to do it now, in case she forgot all the words by morning.

At last she knew she'd finished and she pushed the paper away, spent but satisfied. She yawned and stretched and decided to get ready for bed. It must be well after two in the morning.

But as the weeks went by she found that such moments were rare. The year dragged on at its usual pace. Tim was always there, ever faithful. Except for Wednesday afternoons, he was always at her side. And she clung to him, terrified of facing life alone.

He'd been a bit unsure about the Wednesday afternoons at first.

'What do you want to go off then for? We could go for a walk,' he said.

She stared at her hands and then flung her chin up. 'I want to go. I've joined anyway.'

'Joined what?'

'The Christian Action Society.'

'The what!? I thought you said you weren't a Christian!'

She bit her lip. 'Well, I'm not. Only I still feel I want to help someone. And they don't bother about having to go to church or anything.

He frowned. 'You mean you *need* to go to make you feel better.'

But she pretended not to hear him. 'I want to help that old lady!'

He sighed. 'Okay. Okay. Shall I come with you?'

'No,' she said. 'No. I'll be better on my own.'

Later she sat on the bus and watched as the university buildings slid past, then the smart town centre and at last the tiny, huddled houses on Dewsbury Road. Annie Marlow's corner was coming up and Jenny jumped off the bus and leaned into the wind. Funny how there always seemed to be a wind blowing dust in her eyes round that corner.

She knocked on the door and went in. Mrs Marlow wasn't there. Jenny looked round the room. A fire sputtered in the black-leaded range. The bed was neatly made. She peered into the windowless kitchen. No one there. All at once she heard a shout, 'That you, Jenny?'

'Yes.' She turned round and opened the cellar door.

The old lady was on her hands and knees, half climbing, half crawling up the stone steps, humping a bucket of coal in front of her. Jenny made to help but Mrs Marlow shouted, 'No! No! Don't want you down here! Get back into t'parlour!'

At last she hauled herself into the room, dragged the bucket to the fire and plumped down into her chair. Her hands shone with coal dust and her face was yellow. Her eyes glared for a moment round the shabby room, the peeling walls and her dirty apron. Then they softened as they rested on 'her' university student. 'Get us a cuppa tea, love,' she said, and threw her head back with a bellow of laughter, giving Jenny a shove towards the kitchen.

Jenny grinned. But her smile faded as she waited for the kettle to boil. Fancy a poor, old lady having to crawl down the cellar for coal, and live in a back-to-back and walk right round the row of houses to the next street if she wanted to go to the toilet. Jenny sighed. Where were Annie Marlow's relations? Her friends? Her adopted son?

'Come on, love! What we waiting for?' came the voice from the next room.

'Coming,' said Jenny.

'Well bring them chocolate biscuits as well. And if you don't getta move on, it'll be Christmas!'

All too soon Jenny returned to the Hall. And Tim rang up. And yet another friend bounced in to dinner sporting a diamond ring on her engagement finger. It was quite the thing that year to get engaged and Tim was becoming insistent that she should have a ring. But something in her, something she did not understand, made her unable to make the decision.

One Sunday morning she managed to go out for a walk on her own. As she meandered down the quiet lanes, she saw that the tarmac was blue where the sheet of water covering the road reflected the sky. She stood still for some time and watched the blue road. Suddenly she lifted her head and listened. There were bells ringing out across the fields. At once she turned and her pace quickened as she went down unknown lanes in search of the bells, as if summoned. At last she found the church. She slipped in and sat down, waiting to see, to hear, to understand.

But she heard no message. Received no help. No revelation. Biting her lip hard, she tried to edge away at the end, but the vicar was too quick for her. Even as he talked and tried to draw her out, her own questions clanged so loudly in her mind that she couldn't hear him properly. At last she escaped and ran, as if pursued, away from the building.

In early summer Tim invited her to the Devonshire Hall All Night Ball.

'You play croquet at dawn,' said Pam, 'and then have breakfast. Lucky thing!'

When the evening came she stroked on gold eye-shadow with a tiny brush, and then put on a long, shimmering aquamarine dress. At precisely half past eight she heard Tim's footsteps striding down the corridor. He knocked and she waited for a few moments. He was smiling as she opened the door, and gave her a small cellophane box. Inside was an orchid. With fingers trembling with excitement she pinned it on her dress.

'Come on,' he said. 'I've got a taxi waiting.'

At first the evening went well, but, as it wore on, she found herself staring round the room, searching amongst all the people, searching and looking. Not finding. She tried hard to avoid catching the eyes of any of the Sociology group, who were all older than she was, and friendly with Tim. There was one in particular, James, who never actually looked at her, but always at some space just above her head. But James had seen them. He sauntered across the floor, nodded at her and put his hand on Tim's arm. 'Come on, you lovely people,' he said and steered Tim over to his group. Jenny allowed herself to be taken by Tim's other hand. They sat at a table covered in beer glasses. Tim laughed and chatted easily with them, all post-graduates, some lecturers. She sat in a pool of quiet, her fingers playing with the stem of her wine glass. She let their conversation flow round her, half listening.

Suddenly Tim stood up and pulled her with him. She was silent and listlessly moved round the floor. After a while he said casually, 'I asked James what he thought about your ideas of having a Christian world view without actually being a Christian.'

She looked up. 'Oh yes?'

'He said that someone as young as you couldn't have the faintest idea what a world view was.'

She opened her mouth and then closed it again. An angry flush appeared on her cheeks.

'So please don't bother any more about those questions, will you. Will you?' She forced her eyes to meet his and put her mouth into a smile and folded herself into the dance.

So they danced the night away, and played croquet on the lawns at dawn and then yawned over bacon and eggs. But when she got back to her room and shut the door on Tim, she leaned back against the door-frame with tears sliding down her cheeks.

Why, oh why, wouldn't the questions leave her alone? What was it she was searching for? And why, she asked herself again and again, why couldn't she find it?

Later that week she sat, alone, in her room. She ran her hands over the great shelf of second-hand books. She counted them once. There were two hundred on the second-year honours list. She sighed. She had ploughed through them all, but somehow none of them seemed to have anything to say any more. She glanced at her watch. Not enough time to start her essay before dinner. And she didn't feel like writing any poetry. Things had palled on the English course.

She set off once again down the lanes. In spite of the sunshine and the birdsong, darkness seemed to surround her. It seemed to wait in the wings, with the utmost patience, until the time came to swallow her up. She shuddered and pushed the horrible idea away.

She picked a few wild flowers and suddenly realized she was near Adel church. She walked down the path and then stopped. She looked up at its Norman arch and chevron markings. She stood still for some moments. Then she turned to go. After all, the door was bound to be locked. Halfway down the path she turned round and looked again. A yearning that she did not understand ached in her chest and slowly, ever so slowly, she walked back down the path. Perhaps, perhaps if she stepped inside for a moment....

She pushed the door and it opened easily. She slipped inside and waited for her eyes to adjust to the cool dimness. She walked down the little aisle, stopped at the rail and gazed up at the window. It was beautiful. Her mind said it was beautiful. And that was all.

All at once she began to tremble. She shook from head to foot. Great sobs she didn't understand shuddered through her body. She fell to her knees. She buried her head in her hands. 'What are you?' she said without words. There was no reply. After a while she got up. She walked to the lectern and saw the Bible was open. She read, but it made no sense. Just as suddenly the sobs started again. She searched wildly through her pockets. 'What can I give you?' she heard herself whisper. She had nothing. No money. Nothing. She looked round desperately. Surely there was something. Then she saw her wilting bunch of wild flowers.

That was all she had. She laid the flowers carefully at the altar rail. Then she stepped back. They looked poor and withered. Slowly she raised her head and looked steadily towards the empty church. It was all she had.

When she got back Tim was there, waiting for her, his fingers drumming on her chair arm. 'Please,' he said, before she had time to sit down, 'please make up your mind about me. I'm fed up with all this waiting.'

'But my father said....'

'I know what your father said and I'll wait. But why won't you say yes? You never have, you know.'

She raised her head and stared at him. His face was taut. Slowly she moved her head from side to side. 'I don't know. I don't know. I just can't decide...give me more time.'

He leapt up, flung himself out of the room and slammed the door. His footsteps shattered the silence of the peaceful corridor. She leaned her hot cheeks against the cool window pane and watched him march off down the drive. What was it that was stopping her, she asked herself again. But there was no answer.

In the evening he rang up and apologized. She rushed out and caught the late bus and they met near his flat. They ate fish and chips out of the paper and then went back and listened to Gustav Holst's 'Planets Suite' on his record player. On the way home in the taxi she let out that she was going away for the whole summer. 'My Aunty Mary arranged it,' she said, prattling on faster and faster, 'through friends at their church. I'm going to be an au pair girl. In Finland. They say it's beautiful there.'

Silence settled between them.

'I meant to tell you before,' she said, 'only I....'

His face was set. 'Yes?' he said.

'I, er, thought you might miss me.'

He let go of her hand. 'Oh, I'll see you when you get back, I expect.' His words sounded extra crisp and he sat very straight for the rest of the journey.

CHAPTER FIVE

THE FINDING

At last, like a sailor who perceives
some distant rock after weeks
at sea,
is quickened and toils to reach
land,
so I found him proved.

But as I drew nearer, saw to my
surprise,
it was no barren rock arising from
the northern seas,
but the appearance of green domes
and delicate cupolas,
with light reflected on the cobbled
streets below;
which had always thrived. While I
had tossed alone on alien seas.

The Search
Jenny Cooke, 1977

One morning in early July Jenny stood on the deck of the 'S.S. Maria Ulianova' and watched the Thames estuary slip away, as the Russian cruise boat set her nose for the Baltic Sea. And all her problems with Tim and with herself, and all the darkness, seemed to slip away too, and be left behind in England. She was free on board the ship.

Nothing in her life before had quite prepared her for the endless excitement of leaning over the ship's railings and watching the sea. The horizon was like one huge oval with the sun basking in the bowl of the sky. She drank it in for hours. Sometimes other passengers joined her. Occasionally they saw a barren island rising out of the sea. 'Land ahoy!' they cried and everyone rushed to gaze at the bleak, black rocks.

On the fifth day Jenny got ready early at the prow of the ship and waited. At last the sun seemed to gleam on something far away on the horizon. She leaned forward and then gasped. Far away, but perfectly visible, rose up a green dome shining out of the sea. Other domes and cupolas followed. She gazed, spellbound. At last she made out what they were—the green copper domes of a great building that seemed to rise out of the sea to greet her, from the flat land of Finland.

It was about three weeks later that Eeva, the mother of 'her' family, invited her to a Bible study at the home of one of their aunts. So they were all Christians! At first Jenny couldn't believe it. This Finnish family had none of the drab way of life and dull clothes she'd always associated with Christians in England. None of the safe taste, no 'Present from Blackpool' stuck up on a Thirties mantelpiece.

She accepted the invitation to the Bible study and sat through the impassioned meeting, not understanding a word of the language. But for once she was at peace with herself. And they accepted her, didn't try and push her or make her decide anything. After that she watched them carefully. They ran their farm and gathered in the hay, while she and their three young children bathed in the lake, cycled through the woods and sweated in the sauna. Wherever she looked outside, the silver birch trees seemed two hundred feet tall with cascades of golden leaves reflected in the still lakes. Everywhere were lakes and trees shining in the endless sunshine. She drank it in, hardly believing such beauty was real. And wherever she looked inside, the white, wooden farmhouse gleamed with shocking pinks and turquoise blues that mellowed in the light of the candles they lit every evening.

'Your home is so beautiful,' she said to Eeva one afternoon.

Eeva smiled. 'We like it,' she said. 'It's the new Finnish designers. We like to buy their work.'

The grandmother of the family asked Jenny to lunch one day in her small wooden house further down the lakeside. Jenny asked her about her life. The old woman's eyes smiled but her mouth was firm: 'My husband was a missionary. He went to Japan and I had to follow him later with our baby son. I travelled three days overland to get to Japan.'

'Three days?'

'In the railway. Across the Steppes.'

'How exciting!'

'No...it was boring. And the baby cried.'

'Like Gladys Aylward.'

The old woman frowned and shook her head. 'Who?' she asked. Then, 'My mother was a writer. She wrote many books,' and she gestured towards the bookshelves. Jenny's eyes followed. She saw the neat row of books. A body of work done by an unknown woman, and in her own heart something stirred.

One evening the family went to a village dance. She listened, entranced, as the accordionist played and perspired all night. The sun scarcely went down in the still twilight before it rose again. 'The land of the midnight sun,' Eeva called her country. In between the hectic dances Jenny slipped outside and stood by the lakeside. The water was pink in the setting light and a breeze wafted the silver birches and their tiny leaves. The air seemed to stand in columns between the trunks.

Suddenly she heard a sound of singing and round the curve of the lake came a boat, studded with fairy lights and full of singers and dancers. Slowly it drifted past her and then, just as suddenly, it was gone. She was gripped by an anguish so keen that she had to lift her hand to the rough bark of a tree to steady herself. The boat had been so much here. So real. So alive. And then gone. Snuffed out. She put her hands to her ears, but not before she remembered some words her English tutor had once told them all: 'The Anglo-Saxons said life was like a sparrow flying in from the dark, into a brightly lit feasting hall. It flew past all the revelry and joy on out into the dark again. It flew from the dark, through the light, out into the dark again.'

She pressed her hands over her ears and ran back into the dance hall, terrified of staying alone any longer. If only I could be like the Finnish grandmother, she thought. Strong and secure. But she knew she couldn't.

Too soon, it seemed, it was time to return, to board the Russian liner and stare at the hammer and sickle on the funnel, to lean over the rail and wave to her Finnish friends for one last time and then, finally, watch the green domes slip into the sea again.

Once they got out into the Baltic the wind blew up. During the night she woke up to find the boat rolling and rolling—rolling deeper than any boat she'd ever known before. And next morning when she tried to walk, the corridor seemed to lurch violently and throw her down. The dining-room was nearly deserted. Eventually she found herself huddled on the foredeck with a few other passengers, all of them willing the fresh air to keep the queasiness at bay.

At last, after about twelve hours, the storm blew itself out. The sun shone, people began eating again and the violinist tuned up in the ballroom. That evening she stood at the edge of the dance floor and was soon whirling round from one dance to another. After a while, exhausted and breathless, she slipped outside and went on deck to look at the night. The door clanged behind her, shutting out the clamour of music and laughter.

She went to the railing and stared out across the sea. It was so dark that she couldn't see the water, she could only hear the swish of the boat as it skimmed along. She looked up. It was velvet dark. The air was warm and she wasn't afraid. She gazed at the stars. She felt dwarfed by them, powerless in the midst of all those infinite spaces and remote order. If only she could stretch out her arms and embrace it all.... She lingered on, waiting for the familiar feeling of anguish to grip her, to tell her that all the stars were meaningless; and so was the universe and so was she.

But instead of the anguish she felt a curious quietness within herself. And then a thought hit her. It came so much out of the blue that she was startled into silence.

'And how,' said the thought, 'could all those stars happen by chance?'

How indeed? She frowned and shook her head.

'How could they all move in their infinite pathways, in their orderly way, by chance?'

She waited.

'It wouldn't make sense, would it?'

She shook her head. She remembered someone at school once saying that it would take a roomful of monkeys a million years—or was it a million million?—to mess about with typewriters and produce, by chance, the works of Shakespeare. She looked again at the stars. If it would take that long to crib Shakespeare by chance, how on earth could the universe and all its complexity happen by chance?

'In fact,' said the thought, 'to believe that all those stars happened by chance would take too much faith. Wouldn't it? Wouldn't it!'

Too much faith! Too much faith in chance! She felt like giggling. She, who'd always argued with the ones who had faith, was now in the process of having too much. She looked again.

'So you see,' said the thought, 'you can't be sure. You can't be sure there *is* a God who designed it all.'

She gripped the railing tightly.

'And you can't be sure there *isn't*. You can't be sure one way or the other.'

Suddenly the door opened and the clang of music shot out into the night sky. 'Come on!' called her partner. 'I'm waiting!'

In a daze she turned obediently and followed him into the ballroom. Her feet danced and her face smiled but her mind was elsewhere. As the voyage proceeded and England came nearer, she became aware that her mind was free in a way it had never been.

And before she disembarked she knew something else. She hadn't got that enormous amount of faith and confidence to believe in 'chance' any longer. She lifted her chin up high and watched as the boat edged its way down the Thames estuary. She'd decided to believe in God after all.

CHAPTER SIX

THE FOUNDING

But found…
He was a self both good and
terrible.

Jenny Cooke, 1977

JENNY TOLD TIM about her new belief one Sunday afternoon in her room. She talked and talked, while he simply stared. At last her words staggered to a halt. He sat still, his hands hanging loosely over the chair arm.

'Well! Say something!' she said.

He said nothing.

'Go on.'

He cleared his throat and looked her in the eye. 'You've been through all this before.'

'Yes, but....'

'Why does it mean so much to you?'

She stared at her hands. 'I don't know. I don't know. I feel like I must know the truth. About the universe. And everything.'

He sighed and stood up. 'Why can't you be like other girls?'

She bit her lip. 'I *am* like other girls!'

He paced up and down the room and then came and stood next to her. 'It's different for you this time, isn't it?'

'Different?'

'Yes. I've listened to you talking about the meaning of life so often. I thought you'd grow out of it. You know, a teenage obsession.'

Colour flamed in her cheeks, but he silenced her with the thrust of his words. 'I told James about it and he said you were far too young to know what you were talking about!'

'You've told me that already and I think he's got a cheek. Who does he think he is, anyway!'

'Senior Sociology Lecturer.'

'Hummmph!' And she stumped over to the window and glared across the courtyard.

'Anyway,' he said and his shoulders sagged suddenly, 'I can see it's different this time. You mean it.'

She ran to him and said, 'It needn't make any difference to us, need it! Need it?'

He stared at her, smiled, and shrugged his shoulders.

One evening a few days later she and her friend Angie got back late for supper. As she slipped to the table for the late meal her heart sank. All the church lot were sitting round, talking earnestly. She squared her shoulders and ate her dinner in silence, shutting her ears to their enthusiasm.

There was a movement beside her. 'Terrible this business in Vietnam, isn't it?' Jenny looked round and saw a dark-haired girl she hadn't noticed before.

'Yes. Yes it is,' said Jenny.

She watched the new girl as she bent her dark head over her plate for a moment, eyes closed, lips moving. Jenny saw the copy of *The Guardian* neatly folded by her plate. Then out of the corner of her eye, Jenny saw Angie begin to smirk as the girl said grace. Angie opened her mouth. The new girl calmly began to eat her supper and Angie closed her mouth again, her face puzzled.

Jenny leaned forward and said, 'I saw a photograph in one of the Colour Supplements the other day. It was of a Vietnamese soldier. His face was all creased up. He was carrying his dead child wrapped up in corrugated cardboard.'

There was a silence.

'I can't get that man's face out of my mind.'

The girl put down her knife and fork and picked up her newspaper. She pointed to a headline. 'I can't forget it, either,' she said. 'I keep thinking about it.' After that the two girls got into a deep discussion. Eventually Jenny looked round. Angie had gone. The church lot had gone. She smiled at the new girl. 'My name's Jenny. What's yours?'

The girl smiled back. 'Sue. Sue Harris.'

It was only later when she got back to her room that Jenny stopped dead in her tracks. If Sue had said grace then that must mean she was one of the church lot. Jenny frowned. Sue didn't seem like the others.

It was late one evening. Tim had gone and Jenny was getting ready for bed. She closed her door and was about to cross the room when she heard a voice behind her.

'Read Joshua One,' said the voice.

Startled, she spun round. Silly! There was no one there. She stared blankly at her door and then rubbed her ears. Had she really heard a voice? No. It must be imagination—that must be it. She sighed and set off for her bed.

'Read Joshua One,' said the voice again.

She stopped once more. She *had* heard a voice. Only, was it something in her mind—or in the room? She began to bite her nails, and stood, hesitating, by her bed. She didn't know what 'Joshua' was anyway.

'Read Joshua One,' said the voice a third time.

She put her hands to her ears and half climbed into bed. But then curiosity got the better of her. She pushed the quilt back.

'What is "Joshua"?' she asked. There was no reply. But she knew.

She walked across to her bookcase and ran her hand across her books. Rabelais, *Don Quixote, A Farewell to Arms,* W. B. Yeats, Eliot and D. H. Lawrence, Beckett and Jean-Paul Sartre. And, of course, Milton. They were all there. All the giants. But no Bible. So there was no point in bothering.

Unwillingly she forced her hand to search more carefully. And there, at one side, neatly tucked away, was the black Bible her grandmother had once given her. She opened it at random and stared at the pages. The Authorized Version English balked her and she began to close it.

'Read Joshua One.'

'Oh, leave me alone,' she said. But she looked at the contents page all the same. And there, towards the beginning of the list, she read the words 'Book of Joshua'.

She turned up the page and began to read. But the words didn't make sense. It was a jumble. She made to snap the Bible shut and quell her disappointment. Then something drew her eye again.

'Be strong,' she read 'and of a good courage:
be not afraid, neither be thou dismayed: for
the Lord thy God is with thee
whithersoever thou goest.'

The words leaped out of the page at her. They shot into her mind like a bolt of light. She read again, 'The Lord thy God is with thee, whithersoever thou goest.' Wherever she went, then, God would be there. She need never be alone again. Neither in time, nor eternity. Never. Never. A friend, for ever.

Suddenly she snapped the Bible shut and thrust it back on the shelf. If only it were true. And the old, familiar anguish wrung her heart. If only I could believe it, she thought. If only I believed it, it would be the most wonderful thing in all the world.

But she didn't believe it. She leaped into bed, pulled the covers over her head and tried to blot out the memory of a friendship she could not accept.

The time came when she had to decide what to do after leaving Leeds. She sent off for all the brochures about teaching courses. As she read through them with Tim, she laughed at one entry. 'Department of Audiology and Teaching the Deaf,' she read, 'Manchester University. Well, that's one brochure I won't need.'

Tim was hunting through the ads in the *Times Educational Supplement*, looking for a lecturing post. 'Shall we try and go to the same town?' he asked, without looking at her.

She pretended not to hear him, but he asked again, so she said, 'Suppose so,' and quickly changed the subject.

It was towards Christmas that one of the church lot in the Hall asked her to their Bible study. 'Please come,' said the younger girl, her cheeks bright pink.

Jenny shrugged her shoulders and turned away, but not before she'd seen Judy's eyes go bright and her cheeks flame. Jenny marched back to her room and tried to stop herself from thinking. But it had to be faced. 'You're mean,' she told herself. 'Fancy turning your back on Judy.' She bit her lip and paced up and down her room.

Suddenly she flung open her door and set off down the corridor. It seemed interminable. And dreary. Her footsteps echoed and her feet got slower and slower. In the end she got to the door of the meeting and raised her hand to knock. Her hand stayed poised and then, with a feeling of doom, she tapped on the door.

Somehow she got herself into the room, refused to look at anyone and found herself sitting on the corner of the bed, in a squash of girls. After a few moments she managed to take in what was being said. She raised her head and saw that it was Sue talking. Jenny listened and finally got the gist. She stopped listening, but sat as still as a stone. Sue talked as if God were real. A real person. Not just a force remote beyond the stars but a real person who cared about what happened in people's lives. She stared at Sue. And then the thought hit her.

Supposing, after all, Sue were right and a personality really existed called God. Jenny's ears began to tingle and suddenly, in her chest, she felt warm. A great warmth spread through her. It could just be true.

She wanted to leap up there and then, but forced herself to wait. The meeting had scarcely ended before she belted out and ran down the corridor to her room. She slammed the door. Suddenly it was very quiet. She walked towards her armchair, then changed her mind and knelt down.

'God,' she began. 'Er, Lord ... God, I....' She paused and looked out of her window. A breeze was ruffling the tree tops. Was it possible she was speaking to the personality who had made those? It seemed too incredible. She struggled on. 'I'd, er, like to believe in you. If you exist.' She stopped again. Supposing she was making a fool of herself. But she shrugged. What did it matter after all? No one was there to hear.

'If you don't exist, then that's it. I won't bother. But if you do exist....' She paused and said firmly, 'If you do, and if you'll be a great God to me and answer my prayers, then... then I will follow you. I will.'

There was silence. No voice. And even the warmth in her chest had dissipated.

She told no one about her prayer. Nothing seemed to have

changed. She hung around with the church lot a bit and even went to the Christian Union Christmas party. Half way through the evening she looked up and was so startled that she stopped dead in the middle of the floor. Tim was standing in the doorway, talking to a man she didn't know. She rushed over. 'I thought you said you'd never darken the doors of this Society,' she said.

Tim grinned sheepishly. 'Oh well, I thought, if I was meeting you across the road afterwards, I might as well come in and see for myself first.' He waved his arm casually around. 'I never expected to meet Pete here.'

'Pete?'

Tim pointed after the man he had been talking to. 'Yes, Pete. He's in our Department.' He lowered his voice. 'The Prof. thinks he's brilliant.'

Jenny looked at Pete. 'Oh,' she said.

The next evening the same inner voice she'd heard before seemed to intimate another name to her. 'Elijah,' persisted the thought. 'Elijah.'

After some searching she found the page and read out:

> How long halt ye between two opinions?
> if the Lord be God, follow him:
> but if Baal, then follow him.[1]

As she read and reread those unfamiliar words, she knew one thing for sure. She had to decide. And now was the time. She had put it off for years. But now was the time.

She pressed her face to the glass window and stared at the twilight. Now was the time. Abruptly she swung round. 'Yes,' she said. 'All right. I've decided. It's yes, Lord. Yes.'

It was a great risk, she knew that. People might take her for a fool. She raised her head defiantly at her reflection in her mirror.

'Yes,' she said again. 'It's yes!'

[1] 1 Kings 18:21

CHAPTER SEVEN

THE FOOL

Jesus said, 'The Kingdom of heaven is like this. A man is looking for fine pearls, and when he finds one that is unusually fine, he goes and sells everything he has, and buys that pearl.'

Matthew 13:45–46

JENNY STOOD AND stared round her study bedroom and then looked at her watch. Over an hour to spare before tea. She'd done everything now except tidy up the College prospectuses. She began to stack them neatly and pushed the one about the 'Teaching of the Deaf' to the bottom of the pile. Her hands lingered over the cover of the Newcastle-Upon-Tyne brochure and she placed it squarely on top of the others.

She remembered the day when Tim took her to the interview there. The sleet bounced hard off the train windows and when they arrived the wind blew cold in the northern town. He waited for her outside the building. When she came out she was smiling.

'Have you got in?' he asked.

She nodded and her cheeks were pink.

'Well?' he demanded.

'Well!' she said. 'They said that if I were to come here, they'd be....'

'Go on!'

'They'd be so pleased to have an English graduate, that they'd pay for me to spend a term in America!'

'America!'

'Yes.' She glanced at him. 'Would you mind so much?'

There was a pause. Tim said, 'No, of course you must go.'

She clasped her hands together. 'Oh, I'd love to go! It's only a term. At a sort of twin college there. Oh, I'd love to go.'

There was silence.

Then she said, 'And if, well, if you didn't mind, and if I get my teaching certificate, I'm sure Dad wouldn't mind if I, if we got engaged this Christmas!'

'Engaged!' He stared at her and threw his arms in the air. 'You're not serious!'

'Yes.'

'I don't believe it!'

But she knew by the smile on his face that he was delighted.

Now her hands caressed that brochure again. America! How she longed to go there. And she felt a shivery feeling at the base of her spine.

She glanced round the room once more. Nearly everything packed for the Christmas holidays. Just the brown envelope full of the poems and the unfinished novel waiting to be packed in her holdall. She looked at her watch. Still three quarters of an hour to wait, so she pulled out a chair, opened the envelope and flipped through the poems. One was typed and she reread it. When she'd shown it to Tim, he whistled, 'That's good! Very good. Can I show it to James?'

She grinned as she remembered her reply. 'No! Indeed you can't! It's for the University Poetry Competition.'

But now she frowned as she carefully folded the poem back into the envelope. She wasn't quite sure what it was, but something didn't seem quite right.... It was funny about the poetry, and the novel too. There was a half thought in her mind that said there didn't seem very much left for her to say. Still, not to worry. She stretched, yawned, got up and looked out of the window.

Everything was settled. Her future was secure. Tim had even started coming to church. So why was she so...she shrugged. She didn't know. She tried sitting down again, but was up in a few seconds. She looked at her watch. Still too early for tea. Hilary was out, so she couldn't talk to her. Jenny chewed her nails. She opened her Bible, but no verse jumped out of the page today. Then, as an afterthought, she knelt down by the bed.

She opened her mouth, but before any words formed, she realized that there was another presence in the room; a centre of consciousness other than her own. The atmosphere became charged. The mood of the room changed. She didn't hear any words, only received an impression, a feeling, so strong that it was unmistakable.

'Don't do any more writing,' persisted the feeling.

She stared at her hands. That was the last thing she expected to hear. Did it mean leave off the Poetry Competition? Stop writing altogether?

'But I...' she began. And then she remembered. She already knew really that she had to stop writing, because there was nothing left that she wanted to say.

'Oh,' she said. 'Oh. I see. All right then.' And she rose to her feet, already intent on packing away the poems. But the intensity of that Other increased. Jenny stopped. 'One day you will write, many many years from now....'

Jenny sighed, but already she was pushing the brown paper envelope into her holdall. Well, if that was all the people at the Christian Union meant by 'the cost of discipleship', then it wasn't too bad. She knew she didn't mind too much about not writing.

She spent some time tidying up the prospectuses. One of them fell off the ledge and she read, 'Department of Audiology and The Teaching of the Deaf' at Manchester University. No need to bother about that anyway, now she was going to America. All at once she stood still. Surely that Other presence had gone. But no! As clearly as before it approached her again.

'Don't do the English Course at Newcastle,' it seemed to say.

Not do the English Teaching Course! Not go to.... 'But why not? I want to go to....'

There was no reply. Then, into her mind came the strangest idea. She looked again at the open prospectus in her hand. But people would think she was daft. She thought for some minutes and then looked at the 'Deaf' brochure once more. It would do no harm to send off for more details. No harm at all. She frowned and spoke aloud, 'I did so badly want to go to America.'

There was silence.

She dug her nails in her palms. If she screwed herself up very tight, then she might just be able to forget the teaching of English and even the American trip. She realized almost at once that she would never forget. But she could choose not to go. If that was what this Other, this God, wanted, then he'd have to have it. Perhaps there was something else in store. She sighed. 'All right,' she said at last. Tim would be pleased if she didn't go to America.

Tim! Suddenly she turned round and faced the Other. No, she cried soundlessly and put her hands over her ears. No. She tried to leave the room but somehow her legs walked to the bed and she knelt down. She buried her head in her hands.

'No,' she said. 'He's going to be my husband.'

The Other seemed to stand in front of her and pierce her like a column of light. 'If you leave this husband you've chosen, I'll give you another husband.'

'No!'

'If you leave him, I'll give you another husband.'

She leaped to her feet, clenched her hands and then flung herself on the bed. 'No, I won't,' she said. 'And anyway, who do you think you are!'

The Other waited. Then he said, 'Leave him.'

She stood up. 'But I'm twenty. I've made up my mind. I won't leave him.'

She sat on the bed and tried to think. Light had gashed through the cosy life she'd planned for herself. And it hurt.

'Can't you be satisfied if I give up writing, give up teaching English and give up going to America? Won't that do? That's enough for anyone. Give up this! Give up that!'

The room was quiet. 'Leave him,' said the Other.

'But why should I?' She thought about the possibility of leaving Tim; of having to 'go down' with no ring on her finger. She groaned. She would be alone. Hardly any decent young men went to church. She'd never meet anyone else. She'd be alone. Alone. Alone. The thought appalled her.

Tim still said he was an atheist, but if he came to church more.... 'I'll work on him,' she said to herself, half hoping God was listening and that would be enough for him after all.

'Leave him.'

She heard the words ringing in her ears.

'Leave him.'

The room was filled with the dreadful possibility.

She got up slowly and stuck her chin out. 'I'll do the other things for you,' she said clearly, 'but I will *not* leave him. I've made my mind up. I'd be a fool to do otherwise.'

She crossed the room, opened her door, gave a backward glance and then, quickly, decisively, shut the door behind her.

In the week that followed Jenny put the packet of poems right away and never sent the best one to the competition. She sent off for a prospectus to the Department for Teaching the Deaf and visited a Special School.

After Christmas she went to Manchester University for the interview, determined to make a fool of herself, so that they wouldn't offer her a place. When Mr John, the senior lecturer, asked her why she wanted to teach the deaf, she swallowed, fixed her eyes on the square of window to the left of his head and said, 'Well I, er, became a Christian recently, and it came to me very strongly that this is what I should do.' Her voice sounded flat and unconvincing. She struggled on. 'I feel strongly drawn to it. A voice seemed to tell me....' Her cheeks suddenly flamed and she stared at her knees.

Mr John cleared his throat, 'Did you ever want to do it before?'

'No'

'I see.'

Her hands gripped the chair and she bent down to pick up her handbag. He'd think she was daft, she knew that. A real fool. He was frowning and silent, so she got up to go, aware of the fact that she wouldn't be getting a place there. He looked up but didn't meet her eyes. 'We can offer you a place,' he said at last.

'A place?'

'Yes. On the Course.'

'Oh. Oh thank you.'

'Will you write and confirm it, please?'

She nodded and then escaped from the room, her head reeling.

When she got back to Leeds she wrote off and accepted the place. Then, slowly and sadly, she wrote and cancelled her 'English' place and the American trip. Surely that would satisfy this God she'd decided to believe in.

A few weeks later the unthinkable happened. Tim came round and said, 'I've become a Christian!'

'What!'

'A Christian.'

'Just like that?'

'Well, you know Pete? He talked to me. I believe now.'

Jenny stared at him and waited for her heart to jump for joy. Nothing happened so she said, 'Oh, that's wonderful.'

The winter opened into spring and Jenny was studying hard for her finals. She'd stopped reading her Bible, because every time she did so, the words 'Leave him' seemed to blot out the words on the page. And if she prayed all she heard were the same words, 'Leave him.'

'No,' she said as before. 'I won't.'

As the weeks went by she noticed that Tim was getting involved with a different Bible Study group from the one she went to. They quarrelled when he refused to leave it. They quarrelled if he went anywhere without her. Once he gave a lift to a pretty, second-year student. A girl in Jenny's Hall was quick to tell her about it. Jenny quarrelled bitterly with him the next time they met.

'You're jealous,' he said calmly.

'I'm not,' she said, and burst into tears.

After he'd gone she looked in the mirror. Her face was white with black circles under her eyes. Her hair was lank and her clothes too tight, her books unread and her essays unfinished.

At last, by the summer, she'd staggered through the work, through finals, managed to pass her exams and get an Honours Degree. Her father complained that she hadn't got a First. 'With your brains…' he began, and her eyes filled with tears.

'I did my best,' she said and her hands trembled.

'Leave her alone,' said her mother. And for once he did.

Tim was evasive when she enquired about his Bible Study group. 'There's someone you prefer there, isn't there!' she demanded loudly. She knew. She'd seen a pretty girl with chestnut hair going into the room once. He was quiet. 'No, there isn't,' he said at last. 'If you'll promise to marry me as soon as you're twenty-one, in September, then there'll never be anyone else.'

She told her friend Hilary about it. 'What can I do?' she said, screwing her handkerchief up into a ball.

Hilary was quiet and then swung her long legs off the bed. 'Wait a minute,' she said, 'while I just go and phone Mum and Dad.'

When she came back she was smiling. She tossed her long, blonde hair out of her face and said, 'Mum and Dad are coming over to take me out to tea in the country.' She paused. 'Would you like to come?'

Jenny stared. 'Do you really mean it?'

'Of course.'

'Yes, please!'

But all too soon the lovely, safe afternoon was over. The decision still waited for her, filling all her horizon. She promised to let Tim know by letter and fled back to her home and her parents. Her father got her a holiday job packing bottles of disinfectant into crates and day by day she went there. She discovered that by evening she was mesmerized by the image of bottles jolting past her. She was too tired to do anything but watch television and too exhausted to worry about God and the meaning of life. And Tim. Still she hadn't written. Still she hadn't decided.

One evening she got home from work and collapsed into the kitchen. Her mum called out, 'There's a telegram for you. I'm afraid I opened it.'

Jenny took the telegram and read it.

'Got lectureship at Birmingham. Marry me September. Or not at all. Tim.'

She folded up the telegram and looked at her mother. 'Mum, what shall I do?'

'What do you want to do, dear?'

Jenny shook her head. 'I don't know.' Suddenly she began to cry.

Her mother led her to a chair. 'Listen, Jennifer,' she said. 'I've been terrified of saying this, because I know you're twenty. But since you ask me, I'll tell you. Leave him. Don't marry him.'

Jenny lifted her blotchy face. Her mother put her hand on Jenny's arm. 'You aren't happy, are you?' she asked.

Jenny shook her head.

'And you aren't being fair to Tim. He's a nice young man. He deserves an answer.'

Her mother frowned. 'I've worried about you. Always on about the meaning of life and sitting on cushions on the floor and asking earnest questions and staying up too late.' She sighed. 'I've prayed for you night after night.'

Jenny stared. 'You've prayed for *me*?'

'Yes, dear. I want you to be happy.'

Jenny said, 'Dad doesn't approve of me getting married, does he?'

'Dead against it.'

There was silence. Her mother said, 'You must ring Tim at once.'

'No! Not at once. Later. After tea.'

'All right. But I insist. It must be today.'

'Yes, Mum.'

Jenny trailed to her room and sat on the bed. She looked in the mirror and quickly looked away. She glanced out of the window at the suburban road. No help there. She looked round the bedroom and ran her hand over the homemade coverlet. 'Oh, tell me what to do,' she cried to herself. 'Tell me.' She stood in the middle of the room. 'Please tell me.'

At once the room seemed different. That Other, whom she had avoided so successfully for six months, was suddenly, and definitely, there. So tangible was her sense of another personality in the room that she bent to her knees. He was so real, as real as any physical object. But invisible.

'You know what to do,' said the Other.

Jenny bowed her head. The warmth and clarity of that other person washed over her.

'But I'm frightened of saying no,' she said. 'I might never meet anyone else.'

The Other said, 'If you want to go your own way, you are free to do so.' There was silence. Then, 'But how can I bless you if you do?'

She waited.

'And how will you ever know what I have planned for you? And for your life? And with whom?'

How indeed? How would she ever know? For a second she

looked the Other in the face. For a moment the full force of all that was love and all that was light enveloped her. She dropped her head again. She knew she couldn't fool this Other, this God she'd chosen.

She groaned. She dragged herself up. First to one foot and then to the other. She turned, her shoulders bent with a weight she didn't understand. She trod heavily across the carpet. She stood at the door and then turned back to face the Other, but with her eyes firmly fixed on the floor.

'All right,' she said at last.

She opened the door and wearily made her feet tread downstairs. 'Mum! I'm going.'

Her mother rushed into the kitchen, the unasked question all over her face. 'Righto, dear,' she said, and put her hand on Jenny's arm. 'Shall I come with you?'

'No. I'd better do it alone.'

'What about your tea?'

'I'll have it when I come back.'

Jenny set off towards the phone kiosk. Her steps got slower and slower and when she reached the pillar box, they stopped altogether. 'I'm a fool,' she thought and her bitterness surprised her. 'I'm a fool. I'm giving up everything and everyone for a God I hardly know. Who might not even be there at all.' Her feet began to move again. 'A fool! A fool!' She stuffed her hands into her pockets. 'And who are you, Lord, anyway? Where are you? How do I know I'm not the world's biggest fool?'

She walked on to the kiosk. She dialled the number. She heard Tim's voice. 'Tim? Hello. Thank you for the telegram. It's great about your lecturing job.' The phone crackled. She swallowed and said in a small voice, 'Tim, I've decided about us.' She shut her eyes and said, 'I don't think we ought to get married. I can't. I'm sorry. I'm sorry.'

He began to shout at her on the other end, but she couldn't take it in, except when he said, 'Tied to Mummy's apron strings, I suppose!'

'I'm sorry,' she said wordlessly into the receiver.

'I'll write to you,' he shouted and slammed the phone down.

She heard the dialling tone and put down the receiver.

She turned and left the kiosk, walking blindly for a moment. Then she set off for a brief walk across the fields, before going home. That was it, then. It was finished. She waited to be racked with sobs, but nothing happened. As she made for the fields, the full force of what she had done hit her. There'd be no ring on her finger. No young man wanting to take her out. Nobody to tell girlfriends about. No one. She'd probably die an old maid. She pulled her jacket closer for warmth.

After a few minutes she found herself standing by a stile, gazing across the fields towards Prestbury. The sun was one huge, red ball on the horizon. All the grass and wheat were tipped with red. She watched it for several minutes and let the beauty sink into her. Then, head bowed, she turned for home. As she did so, the Other was suddenly there behind her. She spun back, almost stumbling into a centre of warmth that drew her in. 'Dear one,' came the hint of a whisper. The world seemed to stand still. She waited, hardly daring to breathe. The warmth spread into her chest and then the Other spoke again, words that etched into her heart.

'Because you have done this for me, I promise, that you'll never, ever, regret it. Never, Ever. Ever. Ever. Ever.'

Silence bloomed around her, a silence so golden and so quiet, that she stood stock still. Then there seemed to be a hand fleetingly on her head and her head seemed to open as someone poured peace into her. It flowed down through her chest, into her heart, and down her arms, fingers, legs and toes. Her whole body tingled with it. All her fears and despairs, anguishes and longings, seemed to roll up into one ball, taking with them all her pain and quarrelling with Tim. They melted away and flowed out of her with that great rush of peace. Then gradually it stopped. The Other withdrew.

She turned and ran for home. Her feet skipped and danced. Her cheeks curved and she began to whistle and sing. She rushed through the back-door and her mother called, 'We're in the front room.'

Jenny went into the front room and stopped dead. Her mother had got out the best china cups and lacy traycloth. The silver teapot was there. On a plate were piled wrapped chocolate biscuits.

Her mother said, 'I thought you'd need a bit of something

when you came in.'

Jenny sat down. She looked at her mother and grinned. Her mother stared back, puzzled. 'I've done it,' said Jenny.

'What did he say?'

'He was angry. He shouted.'

Her father got up and gave her a cup of tea. 'Only to be expected.'

The three of them sat together, the television forgotten. Her mother gave her her own biscuit. 'Have mine. I want you to have it.'

Jenny ate it slowly. Strange—to be eating chocolate biscuits mid-week. And having two in one night! She got up and kissed them both. 'I'll have an early night,' she said.

When she'd gone upstairs, her mother said, 'You know, John, I thought she'd be heartbroken. But she looks better than she's done for ages. Our old Jennifer back again.'

John said, 'She's done as she was told, for once. Though I never thought she would.'

Eunice was quiet. 'It's not just that. Though I know she wanted to please us. But something's happened to her. Something's changed. She was, er, all bright when she came in. You ought to have seen her when she went out!'

She gathered up the plates.

'She'll get even more religious now, I suppose,' said John, shaking his head.

'I don't know about that. But something's happened.' Eunice nodded her head firmly. 'And whatever it is, it's good.'

I

PART TWO

HILLS OF CLIMB

They all went on till they came to the foot of the hill Difficulty, at the bottom of which was a Spring. There were also in the same place two other ways besides that which came straight from the gate; one turned to the left hand, and the other to the right, at the bottom of the hill: but the narrow way lay right up the hill (and the name of the going up the side of the hill is called Difficulty).

The Pilgrim's Progress
John Bunyan

CHAPTER EIGHT

THE SECRET GIFT

But found, despite these
  reliquaries,
he was a self both good and
  terrible.
Demanding the first place. Giving
experience zeniths. Seeming
  capricious
yet not so. Yearning to be found
and reflected in his followers,
as ancient tapestry, when worked
  with gold
reflects the sunshine through the
  leaded lights.

Jenny Cooke, 1977

WHEN JENNY AND her parents drove to Manchester they searched for ages amongst the dusty Edwardian villas on the Stretford Road. At last her father said, 'There it is!'

They parked the car and stared at the blackish bricks.

'Come on,' said Jenny and bounded in. She shot up two flights of stairs and flung open the door of the attic. She heard voices and rushed downstairs again. The landlady was waiting at the bottom. She had nicotine-stained fingers and dyed hair. 'You'll have to share the bathroom with seven others,' she said and shuffled back into her own rooms.

Her mother told her later, 'I cried all the way home in the car after we dropped you. It was so bleak and dirty in that road! And the house...!' She shuddered. But Jenny liked it and soon settled in.

The 'Deaf' course was 'the best in the world', or so ran the whisper in the corridor outside her tutorial room. And she made friends amongst the other students on the course, and in the 'Hall' across the road from her attic. She made more friends than she had ever done in her life before. But, and she frowned as she drank a cup of coffee late one night, there was a snag. The people she met at the Christian Union meetings were lovely. They invited her for endless cups of coffee. They talked and laughed till she was completely happy and felt quite at home. She drained the coffee and then went downstairs to make another cup as she tried to work it all out.

The snag had cropped up again this evening. She recognized its signs: a hush in the meeting room, a serious and reverent look on one or two faces. Jenny looked round. All the sensible ones had left for the early bus. She sighed and sat firmly upright in her chair. They were going to try and persuade her again. She knew it.

'You see, Jenny, the things that happened in Acts can happen today!'

She waited.

'People speak in tongues today. Like the disciples did. And people are healed. There *are* miracles.'

She said, 'But I don't see the point of it all. I never heard of speaking in tongues before I came here. And anyway, all that kind of thing died out after the Church began. It's irrelevant.'

It was quite a speech for her. Her friends looked hurt and changed the subject.

Now, as she waited for the kettle to boil in the greasy kitchen she found herself unable to forget the conversation. She remembered that she *had* heard about speaking in tongues before. It was last year on a Wednesday evening in Leeds.

She and Tim, and Pete and Sue Harris and a gang of others decided to go to a Pentecostal Church meeting to see what it was like. As the bus trundled through Headingley, Pete said, 'Christians at this church speak in tongues. They proclaim God's message. They....'

Jenny interrupted, 'Utter rubbish! Nobody can speak a language they haven't learned. I've never heard of such a lot of nonsense!'

But afterwards, in the meeting, she sat on the edge of her seat, while an intense silence descended into the room. A middle-aged man stood up and raised his hands into the air. He spoke. Strange words fell from his lips. Then, with a quiet dignity, he sat down. Someone else rose up from their seat. They translated his message into English. Jenny frowned. It wasn't what she had expected. Not at all.

Later on, in the bus going home, when one or two people tried to draw her out, she refused to answer, but sat hunched in a corner seat, gazing out of the window.

Now, in the greasy kitchen in Old Trafford, she found she couldn't stop thinking about it. Once when she was five, her father and mother took her to a meeting at a special church they sometimes went to. She sat, swinging her legs, in the boredom of endlessly waiting while the vicar droned on, her hands clasping the tiny paper bag of sweets a smiling-faced lady had given her on the coach. Then as people shuffled up to the altar, everything went quiet. Suddenly a voice burst out into the church. Great words were ringing round the room. It sounded like Bible words. She sat as still as a mouse. What would Daddy do? He said you weren't supposed to speak in church. She stole a glance at him. But he seemed to be praying. She craned round and stared. An old man, so thin and bent that his tummy caved in, was standing with hands quivering in the air, and crying out, 'Thus saith the Lord.... Thus saith the Lord...!' Excitement swept round the church. People leaned to listen. Then it was over. He sat again, slumped on the hard seat, as if spent.

Afterwards she heard Daddy telling Aunty Doreen, 'Old Mr Withers prophesied.'

'Oh, I wish I'd heard it. Oh, I wish I'd come,' said her Aunt, her face bright with disappointment.

When Jenny was older she said to her father, 'What was that church you took me to when I was five?'

'The Catholic Apostolic Church.'

'Oh. Why's everybody so old there?'

'Edward Irving began it. The Irvingites. He had followers. My great-grandparents joined.'

'Oh. I see.'

But she didn't see. Not at all.

She made the cup of coffee and trailed upstairs with it. It was no good. She didn't understand what her friends were talking about, with all this speaking in tongues and prophecy. She sighed and pushed the problem to the back of her mind.

The year at Manchester sped by. She enjoyed the lectures and struggled with teaching practice. Soon it was the Easter holidays. She decided to stay at home and get her essays finished and catch up on sleep.

Then one night she had a dream. In the dream she was watching Sue Harris in Leeds, sitting, head in hands, at a table. Everything about the room was dark and bare. Sue was wearing a drab khaki-coloured dress and her face was hidden. But the feeling that persisted, long after Jenny woke up, was of the desolation and despair in that room. She tried to forget the dream. She couldn't. Its anguish had found a chord in her own heart. At last she mentioned it to her mother. 'I think I'll go to Leeds for the weekend and see Sue Harris.'

'Oh, don't do that!' said her mother sharply. 'You need a rest.'

Jenny didn't reply, but turned and trailed up to her room. Her mother was right. She hardly knew Sue, and apart from those conversations about the Vietnam war had scarcely spoken to her. Jenny stared out of her bedroom window. There had, of course, been that time in the Bible Study when she'd heard Sue talking about God being real. Jenny sighed. It would be silly to go all that way just to see someone she didn't know well. She'd be a real fool....

But as the week progressed the feeling of the dream grew stronger. Her heart ached with it. One morning, before breakfast, she spoke to the empty air in her bedroom. 'If you want me to go to Leeds, Lord, then I'll open my Bible and read a verse telling me to go!' She knew she was on safe ground. There was no mention of the word 'Leeds' in any Bible she knew of. She grabbed the Bible and opened it at random. She looked at the page, half-laughing.

Suddenly the laugh was wiped off her face. She stared at the page. She picked it up and read it again. 'Arise,' she read, 'go to...that great city....'[1] She swallowed. Apart from the actual word, 'Leeds', the message was crystal clear. A flicker of fear passed over her. She decided she'd better not be so clever, next time. And, she asked herself as she closed the Bible carefully, who was this God she had decided to believe in?

When she got to Leeds she found Sue living in a flat, seemingly happy and content. Stumblingly, on the second day of the visit, Jenny tried to explain why she had come. Sue was silent.

'I came because I, er, dreamed that you were very sad...and I don't know what to say...only I, I, I mean, God does love you and...I came.' Jenny stumbled to a halt.

Sue sat on in silence for some minutes. When she finally raised her head her eyes were filled with sorrow. 'You came,' she said.

There was silence.

[1] Jonah 1:2

Sue said, 'I can't explain it, but it's helped. And thanks.'

They were quiet again.

'Thank you for coming.'

It was only later on that another girl told Jenny that Sue had been swamped by despair and that she had been praying for six months for God to show her he cared.

It seemed to Jenny as though she'd only been home a few days, and yet it was time to pack up for her last term in Manchester. She gazed at herself in her parents' mirror and swung her hair out. It was growing quite long now. She hummed a tune but then her eyes drew back to the mirror. Slowly she picked up the hairbrush, yet even as she did so a thought was intruding into her mind. She tried brushing very hard, but the thought would not go away. At last she put down the brush.

'Well?' she said to her reflection.

'You've been guilty of telling God what to do!'

'What!'

'You've been saying speaking in tongues is rubbish. But how do you know?' She stared at her face in the mirror and attempted a different parting in her hair.

The thought persisted, 'Who do you think you are to tell him what to do?'

Who indeed?

She got up and quickly finished packing her cases. Even as she did so, she was readjusting her mind to the new way of thinking. It was true. And she didn't want to be telling God what his business was. She snapped the cases shut and dragged them downstairs. It wasn't as if she minded one way or another. So, if God thought speaking in tongues was important, and St Paul did, then she guessed she did too.

Her Christian Union friends were stunned when she told them she had changed her mind. 'Who persuaded you?' asked Roy.

'No one.'

'But....'

She said calmly. 'The thought just came to me. And I'm not worried one way or another.'

He stared at her. But all she said was, 'I'll come with you

to the special meeting at Bethshan.'

The night of the special meeting came and they sat through an impassioned sermon and long prayers. She hung round until the end and then went forward with a few others for prayer. She knelt down in the row. The preacher came down the row praying and laying his hands on each one. When it was her turn, she waited expectantly. He prayed. He laid his hands firmly on her head. They felt heavy and were quivering. Nothing happened. So he passed on to the next person. A few moments later he returned to her and prayed again. Still nothing happened. So she got up and sat on a chair in the corner.

People said being filled with the Spirit was the experience to beat all experiences. She bit her lip with disappointment. Then she raised her chin in the air. Well, she was going to *believe* God was going to bless her, indeed had already blessed her. And blow whether she felt any different.

They returned late, said their goodbyes and Jenny trailed alone up the long flights of stairs. When she got to her room, her room-mate was already asleep, so Jenny crept downstairs to the bathroom, locked the door, knelt down with her arms leaning on the side of the bath and began to pray. She filled her mind with the thought of God, of Jesus, of the Holy Spirit and tried to worship them. Into the silence she became aware that different words were beginning to form in her mind. Hesitantly she spoke one. Then another. And another. She stopped. Her mind was still full of thoughts about Father, Son and Holy Ghost, but her tongue seemed to have a life of its own. Could this be what they meant by speaking in tongues? It was so calm, so quiet, so...obedient to her will. I can speak, or not speak, she thought, just as I can with English!

Next morning, as she woke up, her first thought was whether she could still speak the strange words or not. She found she could. After breakfast another student gave her and her room-mate a lift. And as Ann weaved her way in and out of the rush-hour traffic, Jenny's heart began to pound. She gazed out of the window at the grey streets. She'd had the same experience the disciples had had, all those years ago at Pentecost. It was the same. She stole a look at the other girls in the car. What would they say if she told them—probably stare and smile faintly, but inside they would think she was daft. So she turned away. But she hugged the secret gift to herself all the same and it warmed her.

A few days later there was a knock at her door. Jenny opened it. A girl stood there with a young man.

'Hello,' said Jenny. 'Can I help you?'

The girl smiled. 'We've come from Bethshan. Are you one of the students who, er, came forward at the meeting?'

Jenny nodded. 'You'd better come in,' she said.

'Thanks. My dad asked us to come round and see if you were all right.'

'Your dad?'

'Yes. He's an Elder.'

'Oh.'

The young man said, 'We do follow-up work.'

Jenny hid a smile. They obviously meant well. 'Yes,' she said. 'I'm all right.'

The three of them stood around for a minute and Jenny gestured to her chairs.

He said, 'Do you understand about salvation?'

Jenny had difficulty in keeping her face straight. 'You mean,' she said, 'Am I a Christian? And if so, how and when did I become one. Am I right?' The girl looked at the young man. He cleared his throat. Jenny noticed the girl had an engagement ring on. Jenny began to talk. She told them about the years of searching, about the darkness and being an atheist. Then she told them about Tim. And about giving up going to America.

The girl said, 'Gosh, I hadn't realized...I mean....'

Jenny said, 'There was one thing I never told anyone. It happened last April. I was on my own at home. Mum and Dad had gone to the shops. It came to me that I had to give myself to Jesus. Tell him I was sorry for all the wrong I'd done. And thought.' She was silent and a shadow passed over her face. 'Ask him to live in my heart and life for ever.'

The girl and the young man looked up brightly. This was language they could understand. But Jenny hadn't finished. 'I really resisted doing this. I've always resisted what seemed to me to be a formula, a pat way with religious words.' She sighed. 'Anyhow, I still felt I had to make some kind of formal declaration to God. So in the end I did. It wasn't like when I wept at Adel Church. It was, well I felt a bit silly kneeling down in the dining-room.' She chuckled. 'But I don't regret it now.'

She stopped talking to them and looked at them. The girl reached for her handbag. The young man shifted in his seat. Suddenly the girl leaned forward. 'Thank you for sharing. Actually we felt really nervous of coming. We're not used to students. I wasn't really very clever at school. But it's been good to talk to you. You aren't like what I expected.' Her words tumbled out in a rush and her face was pink. Jenny stared, puzzled. The girl was tall, good-looking, well-dressed. And engaged. While she, Jenny, only had one decent dress in her wardrobe and her hand was bare of rings.

'That's okay,' said Jenny.

'Shall we come again? I mean, will you need fellowship?'

Jenny thought. 'I've got plenty of friends here. Don't worry.'

'Bye, then.'

'Bye.'

Jenny heard them clattering downstairs. She knew she'd never see them again.

She hummed a tune to herself as she tidied the room. There was one thing she hadn't told them; one thing so deep down inside, so way below everything else. She stopped and remembered. It was the day she had been given the peace just after she'd phoned Tim. Ever since then she'd felt completely different from the inside out, as if peace welled up from her heart and kept her.

Soon there was to be a job for her at the Royal Residential Schools for the Deaf in Cheadle Hulme. And a girl called Margaret Alston, whom she'd known slightly at school, had asked her to share a rented Victorian cottage with her in Wilmslow. Everything seemed perfect. But although she didn't know it, her days of youth were nearly over.

CHAPTER NINE

THERE WAS NO ANSWER

Knowing Christ went on ahead,
I followed after; assuming that
his way would easily be light.

But found the path was set
   towards the
dark....

Jenny Cooke, 1978

JENNY PUT HER hands up to her ears and tried to shut out the incessant noise in the classroom. But the screams, whoops and gurgles followed her wherever she went. Deliberately she took down first one hand and then the other. She made them pick up a hearing-aid out of the tray and begin to check the wires and the batteries. Yes, Carol's aid was all right, but the ear-piece needed washing. She stood up and walked across the room, looking for the disinfectant and the bowl. She waved at Carol, who promptly ran off in the other direction.

Just then, there was a great clattering and crashing and down came the dolls' house as Peter and Mark raced down the middle of the floor, making strange noises with guns. Jenny looked round for the classroom assistant, 'Mrs Dickinson, please will you help me to...?' Yells and bawlings interrupted her. The girls were fighting in the Wendy House, throwing empty grocery packets around out of what had only that morning been set up as a shop. Boys were in a heap of arms and legs wrestling over the gun. She ran to the light switch and flashed the lights for several seconds. Most of the children stopped in their tracks and looked at her. She grabbed the nearest book and called, 'Come for a story.'

Suddenly Jenny grinned and felt quite young again. No wonder they had come so quickly. They must have seen the packet of biscuits in her bag under the desk!

But after ten minutes the children were tired. Their concentration faltered. They had said their pitiful few words. They had to play again. And all the biscuits had been eaten. Mrs Dickinson said, 'Don't worry, Miss Appleby. The other teachers have just the same, er, excitement at the end of the day. And you do get them spellbound with the stories.'

Jenny went pink. 'Thanks,' she said.

As she trudged for the Wilmslow bus that evening Mrs Dickinson's words helped. Jenny tried explaining to her mother the following weekend. 'Mum, I think the children are being naughty, only I don't know how to stop them!'

Her mother thought a while. 'Give yourself time,' she said. 'You've only been there a few weeks.' She sighed. 'And you couldn't have picked a harder job.'

Jenny sat on in the twilight, while her mother made a cup of tea. She thought back longingly to the recent days at Manchester University, with the coffee parties and the shared jokes. Now she was a teacher. But she didn't feel part of the adult banter in the staff-room. Yet once, when she went back to visit friends in Hall, she had felt suddenly much older than her friends, and apart from the cosy Christian Union world. And evenings in the cottage were quiet. The girls she shared with were nice and friendly, but often out. She sighed.

The days of that first term crawled by. She lost her voice several times, but it made no difference to the children. They couldn't hear her, anyway. Her head ached constantly. It was strange. It had seemed so right to come here, but now she was here, she couldn't wait to escape at four o'clock.

But of all the week there was one particular hour that was worst of all. She waited till it was her turn to face the hour. It was six o'clock until seven o'clock in the evening. All normal children were at home then with mums and dads and television sets, all except those who were profoundly deaf and had to go to the Special School and be boarders and not see their mothers and fathers. Some didn't have fathers. Some had fathers in prison. Some had mothers who drank. And nearly all came from far away. Too far to be day pupils.

So she had to face thirty older children, all deaf and some very unhappy and difficult. Yet somehow she got through the fortnightly hour without mishap. Somehow it was never too bad. Then came one cold, December night. The children wanted to play 'Ghosts' outside in the dark. 'No!' she said, imagining them running off across the fields, never hearing when she called them in. 'No. We'll do a ball game instead.'

Roger hurled himself on the floor and kicked his feet in the air. She tried to pull him up. He flung her away. Gingerly she backed off.

'Leave him, Miss,' said one of the bigger girls. 'He's upset. His mother don't want him next week. He's only just found out.'

They played the ball game around Roger, while he lay sullen and sprawled in the middle of the floor. Jenny watched him out of the corner of her eye. She knew his father was in prison. Few people liked him. He was abnormally strong. She flashed the lights and they played 'Statues'.

All at once as the children pranced round, Roger tore off down the darkened corridor. Then she heard a frenzied rattling of chairs and a crashing as each one came hurtling down the corridor. She set off down the dark passageway, her heart thumping painfully. 'Please help me,' she prayed. Another chair came hurtling and she stopped.

'Leave him, Miss,' said another big girl. 'He's in a temper.' The other big boys, ignoring Jenny, sat and yawned in a corner.

Suddenly the atmosphere in the room changed. Girls and boys were running round and yelling. Faster and faster they ran. Into the middle of the group shot Roger, screaming at the top of his voice, a chair held high over his head. He crashed it on to the head of an older boy, who ducked. The chair splintered. Roger grabbed it with one hand and, whirling it round his head, set out for another victim. The girls began to cry. Jenny saw at once that they were terrified. She sprang into the group, aware that she might get clouted by the chair. She knew she was helpless but still ran forward. 'Lord,' she cried in her heart, 'Stop him!'

At that same instant the chair fell harmlessly to the ground. Roger stopped absolutely dead. He stared at her, as if mesmerized. All the children stopped. An utter silence fell. She ran on, grabbed the chair and sat on it hard. She was about to tell Roger off and punish him severely, when a strange warmth flooded her chest. Suddenly she saw Roger for what he was: not a violent, hateful boy, but a pathetic young boy, with a frustrated broken heart, broken home and broken life. She held out her arms to him. He ran towards her and flung himself on her knee. He clung to her and she cradled him. The other children went strangely quiet and clustered round. Even the ever-watchful, untrusting ones crept nearer. A kind of peace fell.

'Miss?' said one of the big girls wonderingly, 'are you going to smack him?'

'No.'

'Are you going to tell Mr Sumners?'

'No.'

'What then?'

'Nothing. It's all right.'

And after that there were never any real problems for her on the special hour nights. But still the days had to be faced. Day in and day out. Why, she thought nearly every day, why did God call me to work here, when I'm no good at it and don't get anywhere? But there was no answer.

One evening she sat on her bed in the tiny cottage bedroom and put her head in her hands. 'Why Lord? When I gave up so much for you, and then had that lovely year in Manchester, why is it so difficult here?' There was no answer. The thoughts buzzed around her mind. She thought of herself, perched on the edge of a hard chair in the staff dining-room, tongue-tied and awkward. Why was she like that? She'd been so good at arguing her case in the Sixth Form. So why couldn't she speak up now and feel at ease and hold everyone's attention? She sighed. She knew without asking what the response was going to be. And she was right. There was no answer.

Once a university lecturer came to observe her class.

'Can you help me?' she asked desperately. 'I don't know what to do with the children.'

He looked at her intently and then looked away. 'But they're happy.'

She waited.

He said quietly, 'Actually none of us really know how to teach them. I came to see if you could give me any ideas.'

'Oh?'

He gestured round the room, to the bright pictures and murals. 'You're doing wonderfully well.'

She watched him go. Back to the Department, no doubt, to write up his report with long words and then chew it over with the students. She shook her head. She wasn't one little bit convinced by his praise.

One day she tried to teach her little class of children the Primary colours. They stared back at her, anxious, eyes tense, faces blank. Suddenly she leapt up in frustration, and swept away the pile of blue toys and the clutter of yellow things she and Mrs Dickinson had spent ages collecting. She threw them into a corner. The children sat dead still and stared. Mrs Dickinson looked up, surprised.

Jenny gripped the edges of the chair hard. Then her gaze softened slightly as she stared back at the children. It wasn't their fault. She'd rushed them. She bent to pick up a toy car. 'Red,' she said wearily. She put it down in a big, red circle chalked on the floor. 'Red,' she repeated. Then she pointed to the heap of blue and yellow objects. 'Not-red,' she said. 'Not-red.'

Rosemary smiled and swung her thalidomide arm in the direction of the car. 'Red,' said the little girl and Jenny smiled, in spite of herself.

'Good girl, Rosemary,' she said.

On the way home she was too tired even to look out of the bus windows. She sat slumped in the seat and stared at her shoes. Why, she thought for the umpteenth time, why am I doing this work? Her mind, once so full of Milton, Shakespeare and Jean-Paul Sartre, was now ringing with one, single word only. Red! Red! And not-red! She trailed down the path and opened the cottage door. 'Oh, why, Lord?' she cried out in her heart.

But there was no answer.

CHAPTER TEN

THE ISOLATE

Oh that I were as in months past,
as in the days when God preserved
me;
When his candle shined upon my
head,
and when by his light
I walked through darkness....

Job 29:2–3

THE NEXT SUNDAY evening Jenny was leaving church after Evensong when a young man bounded up to her. 'You're new, aren't you? Do you want to come to coffee at John Watty's?'

'Yes, all right!'

'Right! I'll fix you a lift!' And with that, he rushed off.

On the way in the car she found out from the others that John Watty was really Dr John Watkinson, who ran a men's Hall of Residence for the university.

When she arrived, she sat on the edge of the settee and listened to the ebb and flow of the conversation.

'Jesus is like the spray from an aerosol can,' said a bouncy woman and several heads nodded sagely.

Jenny shrank from the idea. It seemed far removed from the earnest warmth of the Bethshan meetings. A man near her handed her a plate of biscuits.

'No thanks,' she said quietly. The biscuits disappeared. She was aware that the man kept hovering, but she fixed her eyes on the bouncy woman. After another minute she noticed the biscuit plate at her elbow again. She sat very still and stared straight ahead. The biscuit plate didn't move. At last she turned round and said crisply, 'No thank you!'

The man removed the biscuits and said, 'Have I, er, seen you here before?'

'No.'

'Do you often go to our church?'

'No.'

Silence fell between them.

He said, 'Er, would you like a biscuit?'

'No!' Then, 'Thank you.'

Later, when it was time to go home the man appeared at her elbow again. 'Can I give you a lift?' he said. 'I'm taking Robin as well.'

She looked at him properly for the first time. Conservative, dark suit, hornrimmed glasses, thin on top. And older than her. Definitely older. She hesitated.

'Oh well, all right then. I'd appreciate it.'

There was an awkward pause between them.

He cleared his throat. 'My name's Francis Cooke,' he said.

'I'm Jenny. Jenny Appleby.'

After that there didn't seem anything else to say so they completed the rest of the journey in silence. She was glad Robin was there to fill in the quietness in the big car. When Francis dropped her, he said, 'Shall we see you again at church?'

She nodded.

Suddenly and unaccountably he said, 'Where do you live in Wilmslow?'

She said, 'Oh, Lacey Green,' and walked away into the night.

The next afternoon when she got back from work her landlady came rushing round and said, 'Ever such a nice man called here today and asked if I knew you!'

'What!' said Jenny faintly.

'Yes. Such a gentleman. Said he was passing through on business.' Mrs Bumby's eyes twinkled. 'And such a nice car.' She darted a glance at Jenny. 'Is he a bit older than you?'

'Who was it?' asked Jenny, guessing perfectly well who it was.

'A Mr Cooke.'

'Oh.'

Mrs Bumby waited but Jenny pursed her lips.

'Well,' said Mrs Bumby after a moment, 'he asked me to tell you that now he knows where you live, he'll be writing to you!'

The next day was Tuesday and it seemed interminable. 'Why, Lord?' she questioned yet again as she sat slumped on the bus after the gruelling day. When she wearily pushed open the cottage door there was a letter on the mat. She picked it up and stared at the unfamiliar handwriting. It was on posh notepaper, too. She slit it open and read it quickly. Her expression didn't change. 'Would she like,' said the letter, 'to go to the pictures? Or go to a restaurant for a meal?' She held the letter in one hand. She tried to imagine herself sitting opposite Francis Cooke in a restaurant and failed. She'd love to go out somewhere, though. Anywhere would be marvellous, as long as it wasn't school. But it wouldn't be fair to say yes to Francis when she wasn't really interested in getting to know him. She sighed and dropped the letter on the table. No doubt she'd come up with some polite excuse.

The following afternoon she was on playground duty. Her eyes darted over the yard, ever watchful. Everything was fine. She set off on her rounds again, when she stopped and turned to look. Yes, there was that boy scuffing his shoes on the stones. There was something vaguely familiar about him. She frowned and walked on. But the scuffing boy drew her eyes again. Now she came to think about it, he was always hanging about, never playing with the others. He walked from one part of the tarmac and scuffed. Then to another and scuffed. Sometimes he played with a ball, with an enormous smile on his face. Then the ball rolled away, the smile was wiped off and he began scuffing again. She stared. He reminded her of someone. Yes, someone who had trailed around playgrounds, alone, for years. Suddenly the bell went. Hastily she pushed the memory on one side. She got the children into lines and they forged into school.

Next time she was on duty she watched out for the boy. He was still alone. But why should he be, she wondered, when he wasn't ugly, or fat, or hopeless at games? He was perfectly ordinary. She asked his teacher, who laughed and said, 'Oh, David! He's a very quiet child. Pleasant though.'

'But he's always alone.'

The teacher shrugged. 'You often get that, you know. Just one in a group who stays alone.

Jenny stared after her. When she got home that evening she looked up child behaviour in a text book. Her finger ran down the page. Suddenly one word leaped out: '*The Isolate*,' she read. 'The isolate child is one who never makes satisfactory relationships. He plays alone. No one really knows why this is. The homes of such children are often caring....' She snapped the book shut, placed it carefully underneath a pile of magazines and then sat frozen to the chair. She shut her eyes and her hands clenched in her lap. She saw herself walking, walking, always alone in the junior school playground. She remembered herself climbing up the hill home and Erica Layman saying down her nose, 'Go away! We don't want you.' And at the Grammar School, the hateful dinner times, when she was always watching, always waiting. And no one ever coming. Never knowing why.

She sat on and on in the complete silence in the cottage. The room began to get dark. At last she heaved herself up and trailed into the kitchen. She stared, unseeing out of the window. There was a lump in her throat, but her eyes were dry. Suddenly she raised her head and her chin was high. It wasn't any good squashing away memories like that. They always popped up when she least expected. Anyway, perhaps she'd never know why. And even as she turned sadly away from the window to make some coffee, her chin suddenly raised again. 'I won't give in!' she thought. 'I won't. I won't.'

After supper she tried to read the Bible and pray. But the names on the prayer list became meaningless. 'Lord,' she cried in the end, 'Why? Why, when I was a little girl was I an....' She tried to say the word 'isolate' and couldn't. So instead she said, 'Why is it so hard for me at the "Deaf" School?' But there was no reply.

When the term finally ended she went home for the Christmas holidays, where the family were all gathered. One morning in early January she was awakened in the semi-dark by a lot of noise of laughter from her mother and sister on the landing. As she struggled to sit up her mother came into the bedroom. 'You've got another letter,' she said and dropped the envelope on the bed. Liz burst into the room behind their mother, 'Come on, Jen, open it! Open it!' Jenny groaned and tried to get into a sitting position. She took the letter, looked at the handwriting and recognized it as being from Francis Cooke. Liz giggled, 'Look at her face, Mum, it's from that business man, isn't it? Isn't it!'

Jenny cleared her throat.

Her mother was smiling. 'It's after half past nine, dear.

You ought to get up.'

'Oh no!' sang Liz and tossed back her gleaming golden curls. 'She's not getting up till she's read that letter!'

'Well I'm not reading it with you lot in here!'

Liz grinned and sallied forth on to the landing. Her mother left as well, saying she would make some coffee. Jenny could hear them whispering on the landing. Suddenly the door banged open and her mother and Liz marched in and stood one on each side of the bed.

'Well?' said Liz.

'I, er....'

'Has he asked you to go out with him again?'

'Er....'

'He has,' squeaked Liz and bounced up and down.

Jenny grinned sheepishly. 'Yes, I suppose so.'

'Right,' said Liz and glanced at their mother whose eyes were twinkling.

Jenny began to get out of bed but Liz held the covers tight on one side and her mother blocked the way to the other.

'Will you let me get up!' said Jenny.

'Not till you say "yes" to him,' said Liz.

'What!'

Her mother said, 'It would do you good to go out. It's only a bit of fun.'

'Yes,' said Liz. 'And you never have any fun any more. Hardly any friends. Always moping and depressed. And far too religious.'

Jenny went red

'Struggling with those deaf kids.'

Jenny opened her mouth.

'And you've put weight on!'

Jenny closed her mouth again. Her sister was a gorgeous size ten.

'And,' said her mother, 'he'll take you to a lovely place.'

'And,' said Liz, 'he must be religious too if you met him at church! So you're not getting out of bed till you say you'll go!'

Suddenly Jenny began to laugh. The three of them giggled helplessly over the crumpled letter.

'Oh, very well,' said Jenny at last. 'I suppose I'll go. Once won't do any harm.'

'Whooppee!' shrieked Liz and darted out of the room, closely followed by her mother.

A few seconds later they were back. Liz began rapidly dropping things on the bed. 'Here, you can borrow my scarf and my handbag. And here's a blouse. Oh, and a lipstick. A bit of make-up would improve you no end.'

Jenny lay back weakly on the pillow.

Her mother staggered in with a fur coat, 'You'd look good in this!'

Jenny tried to move from under the weight of their gifts and couldn't. 'I don't know what to say,' she said at last.

'Don't worry,' said Liz. 'And anyway, it's not as if you're going to marry him!'

They giggled and laughed until Jenny began to quite look forward to the new term and the date with Francis Cooke.

But when she'd been back at the school for only a day everything was just the same. And in the evening, after struggling with a new boy called Jim, who destroyed every single game and hit all the girls and hurled down all the building bricks and raced round and round and round, and who was stronger than her and Mrs Dickinson put together, after all that, every shred of confidence she'd pieced together over the Christmas holidays had disappeared. She collapsed on to her bed at the cottage. 'Why is it so hard Lord?' she cried out. Suddenly she tore off her shoes and hurled them at the wall. 'Why!' she shouted. 'Why!' The shoes cracked into the plaster and fell harmlessly on to the bed. She stared, horrified, at the two indentations in the wall. What on earth was the matter with her? She was getting worse than the children. Blushing, she picked the shoes up and put them quickly under the bed. But could anything be worse than this hardness? This hardness of following God? She sighed. Even if she dropped God, it would still be just as hard at school. And added to that burden would be the agony of meaninglessness.

All at once, as if from a great distance, she caught a sense of the Lord's voice: that Other whom she had learned to call Lord. She put her head into her hands and waited.

'You ask why,' came the whisper of a thought in her mind.

She nodded.

'You ask why. And I will tell you. Because it is my will. The hardness is because it is my will.'

She stayed there, seemingly for hours.

Then the thought-voice came again, 'And knowing this won't really help you. But it is my will.'

Then the voice was gone.

She sat and stared at the indented wall. Was she going mad? No one ever talked like this at the Church of England she went to. Nor at Bethshan Pentecostal Church. At the one it was all evangelism. And at the other, all the Holy Spirit. They were both right, she knew that, though neither would probably see it that way. But who had ever taught her about the hardness of God's will? She thought back over the long stream of Bible Studies and services she had been to and she couldn't remember ever having heard one word about it. She thought about the Christian Union prayer meetings: the inrush of warmth as the Holy Spirit drew them all together; the sense of being part of something, full of power and love and meaning. It was the most real experience she had ever known. All that had gone now she lived in Wilmslow.

Perhaps when she went out with Francis Cooke the next evening, he might be able to tell her. She thought again of his conservative presence and then shook her head. Nothing for it then but to soldier on. Alone.

CHAPTER ELEVEN

THE SIGN

Conventions moulded you. You
  needed them
with a father at the war.

Public School unearthed the
  talents in your hands,
taught you sport and confidence.

But at Seminary they failed you.
  God needs
academics, not carpenter's hands,

They said.

For F.T.C.
Jenny Cooke, 1976

WHEN THE SPECIAL evening came Jenny was ready early. On the dot of seven o'clock she heard the knock at the door. When she opened it she was surprised to see Francis had shed his dark grey suit for a rich fawn, with a natty silk tie. 'Oh, hello,' she said and led him inside.

The evening passed in a blur of being driven fast in his posh car to Manchester, seeing 'Oliver', eating chocolates and discovering there was nowhere to put a fur coat in a cinema.

'I'll look after it for you,' said Francis and piled it on his knee, where it sat like a hot hedgehog for the rest of the performance.

On the way back she suddenly launched into telling him all about her faith, her answers to prayer, her time in Manchester. But she didn't mention the Bethshan experience, nor the problems at school, nor her questioning. He was very quiet while she talked. Afterwards he said, 'I always did believe God was like that really. Only no one else ever talked about him as if he were real. And, well, over the years everything sort of died inside me.'

'What do you mean?'

'It was as if I had a fire inside me at the beginning. And somehow it went out, or else nearly went out. I think there is still a spark left.' He was silent and then looked at her. 'If you see what I mean.'

It was her turn to go quiet. Then she said, 'But what happened to make you lose it?'

'Oh, well, years and years of nothing happening.'

'But didn't people help you?'

He sighed. 'Not everybody is kind,' he said. 'And anyway, they've got their own problems.'

When she got back to the cottage she found, to her surprise, that she was hoping he'd invite her again. And when he did, she promised to meet him in a fortnight. After he had driven away, she sat for a long time by the dying embers in the front room. He said he'd almost gone like those embers. She shivered. Wasn't that how she felt, really, at the 'Deaf' school—now life had stopped bouncing from one student coffee party to the next; now no one seemed interested in the Holy Spirit—and why she was thankful for even the smallest kind word or friendly gesture? She blushed as she remembered how she had felt about Francis at the beginning. And it was funny how much she had enjoyed the evening, in a quiet, easy way. He wasn't what she'd expected. No, not at all.

In the weeks that followed they went out somewhere every week. So, somehow, with that to look forward to she found herself coping better at school. One Sunday morning he called for her and took her to church. There was a visiting preacher and Jenny settled back into the pew to listen. Suddenly she was on the edge of her seat. 'There are some people,' said the preacher, 'who believe in what has been called "the baptism in the Holy Spirit". Well, frankly, I'm glad I don't count myself as one of them....' He ploughed on while Jenny stared blankly in front of her.

Afterwards Francis said, 'That was a good sermon, wasn't it?'

She didn't reply.

'Didn't you think he spoke well?'

'Er....'

'Come on, what did you think?'

'I, I'm not sure. He certainly spoke very passionately.'

'But you didn't agree with him?'

'Well there has to be freedom of speech!'

She got into the car. He didn't start the engine at once, but leaned back in his seat, with a twinkle in his eye.

She bit her lip and then said all in a rush, 'I'm afraid I happen to be one of those unfortunate people who have had the experience he was so against. And at Bethshan too!'

There was a long silence. She guessed what he would say.

Anyone as conservative as Francis Cooke was bound to disagree. She made up her mind not to argue.

'Well,' he said at last. 'Well, I never did! I've always wanted to meet someone who'd had the pentecostal experience! And then I could find out more about it!'

'Pardon?' she said faintly. She turned and looked at him properly, as if for the first time. 'I never thought you'd say that!'

'Do I look so dyed in the wool?' he asked, and she burst out laughing.

He said, 'When I was in the R.A.F. doing National Service, I was hitch-hiking home one day. A lorry driver stopped and gave me a lift. He was a rough diamond! The first thing he said to me was, "Are you a Christian?" and when I said "Yes", he shouted "Praise the Lord!" and began singing in a foreign language at the top of his voice. After a bit I said, "What language is that?" and he said, "Speaking in tongues!" Ever since then I've wanted to know more about it. Only no one seemed to tell me. Then when I nearly became a vicar, they never discussed it and it dropped to the back of my mind.'

She looked round, startled. 'Nearly became a vicar?'

'Yes. They wouldn't let me carry on with it.'

'But...but...why not?'

'I failed my exams.'

Into the silence, she said, 'Oh, Francis, how awful.' And she put her hand on his arm.

His face softened. 'Don't worry. It's nearly ten years ago now. I came to terms with it ages ago.'

'But...did you feel awful?'

'Terrible. I had to come back here. Everyone had seen me off from the church with such a lot of encouragement. Then I had to return. With nothing. No piece of paper to say I was good enough. But, well,' he shrugged. 'I had to do it. I had to face it. Life has to go on.'

'But what did people say?'

'That was the worst of it. They didn't say anything. They sort of half met my eyes and didn't mention it.'

She thought of her own anguished questioning of God over her problems at school. Yet there had been no question of her failing her exams. She said, 'But how did you carry on, with your faith I mean? Did you feel God had let you down?'

There was a long pause. 'No,' he said at last. 'No, strangely, I didn't. I felt I'd let him down. But,' and he sighed, 'life passes. I found a job as a salesman. So here I am.' Suddenly he seized her hand and kissed it. 'And here you are,' he said fervently.

She went home, feeling very worried. He was so nice. He was obviously getting keen on her. But she had to face facts. She liked him very much, but after Tim, she felt very cautious. She sat in her room and tried to think it out. Francis was the first person she'd been out with since Tim. The one or two who'd asked her, she'd refused. She grinned suddenly as she remembered an earnest young man she had met on the Operation Mobilization team in Italy. How he had gazed into her eyes and said that the Lord had told him that Jenny was going to comfort him and become his wife. How she'd managed not to say tartly, 'Well the Lord may have told you, but he hasn't told me!' was something she'd never know!

But what was she to do now? If only the Lord would give her a sign... but then of course he might not want to.... All at once she stopped. The room went very still. Into her mind had come the strangest idea. It was so strange that she couldn't believe it at first. But the idea was persistent. She shook her head. It must be her imagination. She'd obviously got speaking in tongues on the brain. No wonder the church people were unhappy about it. She would have to be careful. But the idea took root. It wouldn't go away. She *was* to have a sign that Francis was the one chosen for her to marry. The sign would be that in the following May he would speak in tongues.

She frowned. It was too much. It really was too much. 'I never mentioned marriage, Lord,' she said. But the idea dug itself into her mind and stayed there. She paced up and down the room and then stopped. 'Right,' she said to herself. 'If God has spoken, it's up to him to bring it to pass. From now on my lips will be sealed as far as "tongues" goes. And as for mentioning the idea of marriage to Francis! That's out!'

A few days later she got a letter. When she saw the handwriting she bit her lip. It was from Tim. Very slowly she opened it. 'I wanted you to know,' he wrote, 'that I have got engaged to Mary. You might remember her.' Jenny stood very still. She remembered the pretty, chestnut-haired girl, who went to Tim's Bible Study group. 'We're planning to get married soon. I wanted to tell you myself before you heard on the grapevine....' She thought for a minute. It was typical of him to write. Very decent really.

Immediately she got a pen and paper and wrote saying how happy she was for them. She sucked the pen a moment and then ended casually, 'I've met someone else too. He's a business man in Manchester.' She realized that she was fiercely glad she was able to say that.

When she got to school she collected her little group of children together and began to teach them how to draw themselves. 'First the face, then the eyes,' she said. She drew a face on the blackboard. Out of the corner of her eye she saw Gerald twisting his fingers in front of his face, a beatific smile on his fat cheeks, while all the time his eyes were glazed. She sighed. She knew she'd never get anything out of him. Another teacher had said he was worse than a vegetable.

She was about to draw the toes on the board when a fight broke out over the crayons. She quelled it and hastily gave out paper. 'Please help them, Lord,' she prayed mechanically to herself and sat down to observe. Jim, she now knew, was able to draw a rough circle and that was a big improvement. Karen drew a tight, little figure in the middle of a huge expanse of white paper. During the relative silence that followed, Jenny noticed something strange about Gerald. His hands had stopped twisting. His head was low over his desk. His tongue was moving in unison with his pencil.

She tip-toed up behind him to have a look.

She stared at the paper: a beautifully drawn boy stared back. Every proportion, every eyelash, every nook and cranny of the hearing aid, were neatly drawn. The whole was an exceptionally good self-portrait, the like of which she had never seen any child draw. Ever. Let alone the 'vegetable' called Gerald. It didn't make sense.

She crossed to the shelf and got down a book on Intelligence Testing. She opened it and ran her finger down the index. 'Drawing the human body', she read, 'A Rough Guide to a

Child's Mental Age'. She looked back at Gerald. He was eight years old and spent all his time smiling, cross-eyed, at his twisting fingers. He sat all day. He rarely moved. He was never naughty. He never played or cried. He was entirely in his own little world. Now he began to twist the pencil in his hands, leaned forward to add a finger nail to his picture and then sat back in his chair. He looked round and for the very first time caught her eye. He beckoned and she walked over, pretending to be casual. He pointed to the picture and drummed his other finger on his chest.

'Yes, Gerald, it's you,' she said. 'It's wonderful.'

A great smile lit up his plump face. He pointed towards her and gestured to the clean paper. She ran for a sheet and gave it to him.

She rushed out of the room and called for the Infants' Head. The two women tramped back down the corridor and stood by the classroom wall, watching him. Jenny did a quick score on the first picture with the intelligence test. She put it down, bewildered.

'It can't be right. He's got no language,' she said.

'What's the score?'

'Eleven and a half years old!'

The Infants' Head was silent. 'If I wasn't seeing it with my own eyes,' she said at last, 'I couldn't believe it.'

They went forward to his desk together. He had finished the second drawing and was twisting his hands together again, the picture forgotten. Jenny stared down at her portrait and began to giggle helplessly. 'He's even got the checks on my skirt,' she said. 'And my hairstyle!'

'And the parting down the right side. And the freckles!'

Jenny said, 'Now what?'

'I don't know. But one thing is for sure. He can't be classed as a "vegetable" any more!'

In the days that followed Gerald did several more of the drawings. He still couldn't speak, nor read, nor write, nor do sums. But he could draw and, somehow, he knew he had done well and began to make friends with the other children. When his mother came to collect him on Friday, she plonked herself down on an Infants' chair and said, 'I always did say that our Gerald was a genius!'

And all the while Gerald was blossoming Karen stood, or sat, tensely still, in her corner. Jenny sighed. She held the child's hand every day and gradually the little girl left off standing quite so rigidly in the corner and sometimes ran across the room and clung to Jenny's hand. But even so Karen was still as stiff as a ramrod at her side.

Jenny remembered the day the Headmaster brought Karen to her classroom door. He pushed Karen in front of him and said, 'Here's a new girl for you. From Wales. She's got no language at all.'

'No language!'

'No.'

Jenny was silenced. Then she said, 'How old is she?'

'She's six. I don't know what's happened to her. She's never been to school either. She can't talk at all. She knows no words. And she's going to be a termly boarder.'

Jenny gazed at the child's white face, the two unshed tears making her grey eyes look enormous.

'Do your best, will you?' said the Head.

'Yes,' she said. 'I'll look after her.'

After a term Karen was still as stiff as a ramrod, still had the unshed tears and still made no sound.

Jenny said to Francis one day, 'She has no idea what a word is! No concept. And how can I teach *that* to her?'

'You can't.'

'But how long do I wait for it to "click"?'

'I don't know.'

'But I keep praying for her. And for the others. But nothing ever happens.' Her voice was bitter. She went quiet and then said, 'It goes through me every Friday afternoon. The parents come for the weekly boarders. The children get so excited. But the termly boarders go and stand about in the hall and try and look as if they're playing. Then, when I walk down the drive home, I look back. And I can see all those children with their noses pressed against the glass windows, watching the lucky ones go home for the weekend. Their faces are wiped of emotion. It's awful.' She blew her nose and said, 'Actually, I had an idea. Could we, I mean, would you mind if we went in your car and took one or two of them out for a picnic on Saturday afternoons? I don't mean every week. But sometimes.' She fixed her brown eyes on his face.

'Of course. Of course,' he said gently. 'I'll do anything for you.'

Next Saturday afternoon they set out for Lyme Park. After the sandwiches and cakes were eaten they settled back on the grass and watched Karen and David Johnson romping up and down with a ball. Suddenly Jenny sat bolt upright. 'Listen!' she said and clutched Francis on the arm.

He looked round, 'What do you mean?'

'Listen!'

He listened.

'What can you hear?'

'... the children. Laughing.'

She threw up her arms in the air and laughed in delight. 'Yes! Yes! Yes!'

'But I don't see...?'

She shook his arm impatiently. 'It's Karen. She's laughing. She's laughing!'

'But?'

Jenny looked at him. 'She's never made any noise for nearly eight months. I've tried. Mrs Dickinson's tried. We've all tried. Tickling her even. But nothing worked. She never had a *voice*. No sounds. And now,' Jenny looked at the two children. They were pink and tousle-haired. 'Now, she's laughing. She doesn't even know she's doing it, but isn't it a beautiful noise?'

He said, 'It means one thing anyway.'

'What's that?'

'She's happy. And that's the best thing in the world for any child.'

Soon it was May-time. Sometimes Jenny remembered the inexplicable sign that had been intimated to her. 'Oh yeah!' she said to herself one day. It wasn't that she exactly disbelieved God. It was simply that she did not trust her own ears.

'I'll do it on Saturday,' said the thought-voice.

She spun round. 'What!'

'I'll give you the sign on Saturday.'

She stared blankly at the wall and pushed the thought

away.

The Saturday came. Francis collected her from extra duty at school and took her to lunch with his parents at Poynton. Mrs Cooke kissed her and took her to the table, groaning with food. The three poodles barked and snapped round her heels and Mr Cooke shyly enquired about her morning. As they sat eating it struck Jenny how absolutely impossible the idea of Francis and the sign was. Such things were not 'done' in his circle. In fact speaking in tongues was frowned on. It wasn't 'balanced', even though it was in the Bible. She'd never mentioned it to him since the day of the sermon and he hadn't asked.

After lunch he invited her for a drive in the country. They bowled along and all at once he said, 'What are you thinking about?'

'Oh, nothing.'

'Yes you are.'

'Well... I can't tell you about it. It's, er, something I thought the Lord told me. It's...' she shrugged.

The silence grew between them. He swung the car into a gate-way and said, 'Jenny, you weren't thinking about speaking in tongues were you?'

Startled she looked at him. 'What!'

'It's only that ever since I got in the car today with you, I've had these strange words rolling round my mind. Every time I think about them I feel really glad and happy and my mind is full of thoughts about the Lord.'

She listened, quite unable to speak.

'Jenny, do you think these words are what people call "speaking in tongues"?'

She sat, incapable of doing anything except stare straight ahead. She nodded. 'Yes,' she whispered at last. Then she looked at him. He was just the same. Solid. Evangelical. Anglican. Conservative. A Son of God. A precious person. A man chosen for her. She shut her eyes and when she spoke her voice was shaky. 'It's wonderful.'

He smiled and suddenly in the happiness that bathed his face she knew that for as long as he lived, she was never going to be truly alone, or lonely, again.

CHAPTER TWELVE

THE WORD

He is your living Word.

The first eucharistic prayer
Alternative Service Book

On the Monday before term started at the beginning of her second year at school, there was a sudden knock at her classroom door. She looked up from amongst the word-charts and pictures she was preparing for her new group and saw Francis through the glass pane.

'Come in! Come in!' she called.

He came in and stood about a bit and then said, 'Would you like to come to Lyme Park when you've finished?'

'Oh yes. What a lovely idea.'

Later as they sauntered round the rose garden, he said, 'Let's go and sit in that rose arbour.'

She followed him, her mind in a dream about the soft blue sky, the pink roses massed everywhere and the singing of birds. They sat down quietly for a while. She became aware of his stillness and glanced at him.

He said, 'Will you marry me?'

A great smile lit up her eyes. 'Yes.'

He took her hand to his lips. 'You aren't worried about me being twelve years older than you?'

'No.'

'And when I told you I'd been engaged before?'

'No.' She giggled. 'That makes two of us!'

The wedding was fixed for the first day of spring. The months flew by in a whirl of activities and preparations. Jenny told him about the sign.

'How extraordinary,' he said. Then, 'You never told me!'

'Certainly not! I wasn't going to do myself out of a proposal! Anyway, how were you so sure it was the right idea to marry me?'

'You won't believe me if I tell you.'

'Go on. Try me!'

'Well,' he said shyly, 'it was that very first night you walked into church. I noticed you. And, of all the amazing things, the Lord spoke to me.'

It was her turn to look shy.

'The Lord said, quite simply, "That's the girl you are going to marry."'

'Honestly?' she said, 'Just like that?'

'Just like that. And, well, I fell for you from that moment on.'

'But what did you think when I refused to go out with you?'

His eyes twinkled. 'You know the old proverb... "If at first you don't succeed, try, try again"!'

And for once, she was silenced.

A few days later she was in the staff dining room and went to the noticeboard to look at the duty rota for the summer term. Her new initials shone out resplendently. She stared at them and a tiny flush crept up her cheeks. Suddenly there was a voice behind her. 'Who on earth's J.C.?'

'It's me,' she said. 'Those are my new initials after I get married.'

There was a moment's silence.

Then, 'How appropriate. J.C. by name. And J.C. by nature!'

The sneer filled the room. She bit her lip hard.

'Do you mind!' she forced herself to reply crisply. Then, as loudly as she dared, she said, 'What a thing to say!'

The door of the room banged and she was left alone. Her eyes pricked. Other scenes rushed into her mind. A friend slamming down her knife and fork and saying, 'I *hate* Christians!' Once in the family circle, a jeering laugh and then, 'She *prays*!' And worst of all, the polite cold-shouldering, the smirk half-hidden behind the hand, the feeling of never quite belonging. Anywhere. Her shoulders drooped and slowly she turned to go. But all at once she raised her chin and stared hard at the slammed door. 'Blow it!' she thought. 'I won't give in! I won't!' Her eyes stopped pricking and she marched from the room, her face carefully set into pleasant lines.

When she got to her classroom Andrew Thomas was yelling and there were a pile of torn papers on the floor. Her cheeks went an angry red and she grabbed for the papers. All the word charts she had made in the holidays were spoiled. Karen ran to help her but Jenny brushed her aside. She got the children into their semi-circle and then turned to Andrew. 'Why have you torn up my new word charts?'

'I didn't. I didn't!'

Wearily she smacked him and took away all his sweets. He sobbed for the rest of the afternoon and she ignored him.

Next morning she was about to open her classroom door when Mark and Peter ran up to her out of their lines. She looked at their set faces. 'What now?'

'Please, Miss, we....' Mark's lip trembled and Peter began to cry.

'What is it?'

They looked at each other. Peter drew in a sobbing breath and said, 'We did it, Miss. We tore the papers.'

She stared at them. 'You! But why?'

'We thought they were old...we wanted to make aeroplanes....'

She walked back to the classroom. Her feet got slower as she neared the door. What was she to do? She'd accused Andrew and punished him. Visions of Billy Budd and 'Mutiny on the Bounty' filled her mind. She put her hand on the door knob and stopped. She'd been too quick. Andrew had a bad name and she had fallen into the trap. It was unjust.

She got herself inside the room. The children filed in and sat down. She gestured to Andrew to come out and he did. She looked at him. He was still white-faced with smudges beneath the eyes. She took a deep breath. When she had done what she knew she had to do, she guessed he'd take advantage of her. It would be difficult for the rest of the term.

'Yesterday,' she said, 'I smacked Andrew. I said he had torn up my papers. I said I wished he wasn't in my class.'

Nine pairs of eyes were glued to her mouth. Andrew's eyes were fastened on hers. She cleared her throat. 'Then I found out this morning that Mark and Peter did it. They came and told me the truth. So Andrew didn't do it. I was wrong. I should have found out properly.'

The children sat as if mesmerized.

She turned to Andrew and held out her hand. 'I'm sorry. Please forgive me.'

For a second he held her glance, his eyes still swollen and brooding, weighing her up.

'I'm sorry,' she said.

Suddenly he sprang up and hurled himself at her. For a moment she was startled and then she felt his arms round her neck. He planted a great kiss on her cheek and rubbing his eyes with his fist, went and sat down. Karen leaped up and grabbed her satchel. Inside were piles of sweets. She shared them round and all the children laughed and chirruped with their strange, deaf voices. In the midst of the party atmosphere Andrew sat smiling to himself, all the fight gone out of him.

Many weeks later, when she and Francis were getting their new home ready, Jenny said, 'You remember me telling you about Andrew? Well, after I said sorry, I thought he'd be worse than ever. And think I was weak.'

Francis put down his electric drill. 'And?'

'He's been as quiet and good as can be. No cheek. I'm really surprised.' She took off her glasses and rubbed her eyes. 'There is one thing though.'

'What's that?'

'I do jump to conclusions awfully quickly. I ought to be more careful. Give people the benefit of the doubt.'

He grinned and said nothing.

It was when the wedding was drawing nearer that Jenny noticed the advertisement in *Renewal* magazine. It showed a hollow-faced child with a distended stomach. 'Send thirty pounds,' said the caption. 'It will feed a child like this for a year.'

Her hand tightened on the purse in her pocket. She pushed the magazine away and went to get a tray of coffee and biscuits ready. Then she went and sat in the tiny front room. She lingered over the coffee and went into a dream about her wedding dress. She hugged the remembrance of the Lord's faithfulness to her. He was giving her the husband he had promised. Life was going to be so exciting from now on, so full, so...she picked up a glossy magazine so that she could pore over the pictures of floaty wedding dresses. She knew she had a little money put by. There was just enough for a super dress.

The *Renewal* magazine fell out along with the glossy. She picked it up off the floor unwillingly and tried to shove it behind the cushion, but not before the emaciated child's face had caught her eye again. A preposterous idea formed in her mind. She sat up straight, biting her lip.

No, she said at last to herself. I've a right to a beautiful dress. No, I'll send something later. All night she tossed and turned. By morning she had made up her mind. She had no idea what she was going to wear in twelve weeks. No doubt something would turn up. She could count on one school pay cheque at least. Slowly she wrote out the cheque. She posted it. She plodded to school. Obeying God did not necessarily make anyone have a good day. She knew that. And her day was as difficult as usual.

A couple of weeks later she staggered in from school and picked up an official letter from the mat. She frowned and opened it slowly. She gazed at the tax form and then turned it over. Neatly clipped to the back was a cheque. She stared at the cheque blankly. It was for thirty-one pounds.

Later Francis explained it to her. 'It's a tax rebate.'

'Oh? I never had one before.' She grinned suddenly. 'I know what I am going to spend it on!'

'What?'

'Not telling you.'

That week-end she rushed into Manchester with her mother. In the second shop they tried they found *the* dress. It was fairly plain and silky, with glossy ribboning at the front. It had two inner skirts and a flowing train at the back.

'It's a really stately dress,' said her mother. 'It suits you exactly. I never dreamed we'd find a dress like this. It's so *right*!'

She searched Jenny's face and Jenny grinned quizzically.

Then it came to her mother-in-law's turn. 'I've managed to borrow you a veil, dear.' Jenny swallowed. Suppose it didn't 'go'? But she meekly went to view it all the same.

'There,' said Mrs Cooke, triumphantly, and held up the veil. 'It's got hand-made lace flowers scattered all over it. I should think it cost the earth!'

Jenny's cheeks went pink. She touched the veil and stared at it as it cascaded delicately and frothed to the floor, the tiny lace flowers showered in its layers.

'It's absolutely...beautiful,' she whispered.

Her mother-in-law's face creased with smiles. 'When I first saw it, I thought it was the loveliest veil I had ever seen.'

And so perfect, thought Jenny, with my special dress. Almost as if the two had been designed to go together.

Her mother-in-law said, 'I was so worried in case you wouldn't like it.'

'Oh, but I do. It's out of this world.'

Jenny sat in a dream on the way back in the car. She hadn't expected to be dressed quite so perfectly.

When the day before the wedding came the staff at school gave her a silver brooch inlaid with paua shell and the children made her an enormous card. On the day itself it rained and rained. But Jenny and Francis didn't care. For her, frothy in glistening white, and him, immaculate in top hat and tails, the day passed only too quickly and soon they sped away on their honeymoon.

When she came back from the glorious holiday spent walking among daffodil fields in the Scilly Isles, the members of staff cross-questioned her about it. She smiled secretively. How to ever tell them about the joy of it all? 'I saw Harold Wilson sunbathing,' was all they could get out of her.

The classroom was awaiting her, just the same as usual, except that a few cork tiles had fallen down from the ceiling. She stood and looked around. Just the same, and yet different. For she was different. And it felt good, being different. The children trooped in, Karen as ever lagging behind. She was taller now, with pink cheeks and bright eyes. Most of her rigid tension had gone. But apart from the laughter at Lyme Park, she still made no sounds. Jenny's throat ached as she observed Karen playing. Six years old and no language. No way of ever telling anyone if she felt sad or angry, happy or lonely. When Jenny tried to make her imitate words, she opened and closed her mouth like a little fish, desperately trying to please; but with no idea why she was doing it.

As Jenny watched her that morning, she remembered seeing a film on television about Helen Keller. She was deaf and blind and her teacher persisted for eighteen months until the child learned her first word at the age of seven. But Helen Keller had had full hearing until she had caught meningitis at the age of eighteen months. She could have had a residual memory of language. Whereas Karen had never heard anything in her life at all. Jenny sighed.

A couple of months later the Head came to her door with a large, brown paper parcel. He gave it to Jenny. 'It's for Karen,' he said. The children flocked round and Jenny began to tell them Karen had got a parcel. Suddenly a strange voice called out, 'Home! Home!'

Jenny stopped and looked round. Whose voice was that? She'd never heard it before. She knew all the voices in that room. Then she saw Karen. The child was standing up in her eagerness, her face quivering. 'Home,' she cried, pointing to the parcel. 'Home!'

She looked as if someone had turned a light on inside her head. 'Home! Home!'

Dazed, Jenny gave her the parcel and then sat back and watched. Karen's learned to say her first word, she thought, and suddenly she relaxed into her chair. After all the work, all the effort, all the ten months of waiting, the child could now say and understand her first word. 'You clever girl,' she said and gave Karen a big hug.

The other children seemed to realize the importance of it. Gerald drew a portrait of her. Jim didn't hit her. The other girls let her play with them. All day long Jenny heard Karen saying, 'Home! Home!' followed by a great gale of laughter. Every time Jenny caught her eye, Karen blushed and then laughed again. In the afternoon Assembly all the children in the school clapped her.

The next day she learned another word. 'Fish,' she called, pointing to a tadpole, 'Fish!' In those last six weeks before the summer holidays Jenny noted down fifty-three new spoken words in Karen's file. And the best of it was that now she was a happy girl, playing with the others, giggling over daft jokes and quite relaxed in the classroom. At the end of the term Jenny decided the children had now got enough language to have a Scripture lesson. She drew a big picture of Jesus and put it up on the wall. Underneath she wrote, 'Jesus loves....' Then all the children wrote out their names and stuck them on the picture. Jim frowned at it. Gerald twisted his fingers at it. And sometimes she saw Karen blushing and staring at it. Jenny smiled tiredly to herself. There was nothing more she could do.

And then, when she was twenty-five and almost into her fourth year at the school, she and Francis went on a late summer camping holiday at Keswick. One day her parents-in-law and brother-in-law joined them for a picnic lunch on the shores of Lake Coniston. The meal went well. Jenny pretended to be as happy as they all were. But waves of sickness kept passing over her. The only time the nausea lifted was while she was eating. She went and stood by herself at the lakeside. She stared out across the water. But she didn't see it. For into her mind nudged the exciting possibility of a new life within her.

PART THREE

CLIFFS OF FALL

O the mind, mind has mountains;
  cliffs of fall
Frightful. Sheer, no-man
  fathomed. Hold them cheap
May who ne'er hung there.

No 42. Poems 1876–1889
Gerard Manley Hopkins

CHAPTER THIRTEEN

THE FIRSTBORN

There was no joy when you were
  born
Dear son. . . .

The Firstborn
Jenny Cooke, 1977

Jenny's pregnancy was confirmed and their new baby was due the following April. The months rushed by, until three weeks before the April date. Jenny stared at the clock on the wall. She felt the tightening in her stomach walls. She looked at her watch. There was the tightening again. She rang up Francis. He came home and together they dialled the hospital number. The sister on duty sounded unimpressed. 'I suppose you had better come in,' she said, her voice flat.

At last Jenny found herself leaning back on the pillows of a high bed in a tiny labour room at the hospital. A nurse gave her an injection and in no time Jenny felt as if she were floating away. As she drifted in and out of sleep she was aware of Francis sitting on her right side, holding her hand. There were also different people coming in and out of the room: doctors, nurses, midwives, students and physiotherapists. And still she floated, as the contractions got closer and closer together. 'It's easy,' her mind seemed to say. 'Easy....'

Suddenly a brusque voice jolted into her dream-like state. 'Mrs Cooke! Mrs Cooke!' She pulled herself up from the layers of easy sleep.

'Mrs Cooke!'

She opened her eyes.

'I'm sorry, Mrs Cooke, but your womb isn't contracting properly any more. We'll have to put you on a drip.'

She looked up trustingly at the doctor. He was young and he was frowning. He said, 'It'll speed things up a bit for you, otherwise you'll be here all night.'

She nodded and held out her arm.

An older woman in a midwife's uniform waddled in. Jenny

tried to smile at her and the woman's black face melted into a big smile. 'Come along, my lovely,' she said and came and held Jenny's other hand. 'Now just you wait for the next pain.'

But when the next pain came it didn't behave like the others. It grew and grew to a peak and then, instead of dying away, it stayed at the peak, growing all round her groin, and thudding. How long it lasted Jenny didn't know. But in the end it slid away. She opened her eyes and stared straight into the black nurse's face. The older eyes gazed back, gently smiling, but behind the smile lay a sorrow. Jenny clung to the calloused hand. 'Is it nearly over?' she whispered.

The black nurse's face never altered, but her eyes seemed to grow sadder before the smile took over. 'You'll be all right, my lovely,' she said. 'The Lord'll help you and you've got a good man here. He'll hold your hand.'

Then, as the next pain loomed, she said, 'It's bad, eh? Never mind. Soon you'll have a lovely baby.'

All at once Jenny remembered reading in one of her childbirth books that a bad contraction could come just before the second stage.

'I want to push now,' she called out.

The young doctor bounded in. 'Are you sure?' he kept asking, between frowns.

'I can't see the baby's head. Are you sure?'

She nodded vigorously.

He ran his hand across his brow. 'All right then.'

The black midwife put her head round the door. 'Good luck, my lovely,' she called. 'I've got to go home now. It's getting late.'

Jenny looked at the clock. It was twenty past eight in the evening. She had been in the labour room for just over five hours.

She was wheeled on a trolley to the delivery room, with Francis on one side and a nurse on the other. The new room was bigger and the walls covered with glass cases with shiny instruments in them. Quickly she turned her head away from the walls and concentrated on her body. It was half past eight now. Soon it would be over. The physiotherapist at the relaxation classes had said that no doctor would ever let a mother stay in the delivery room for any longer than an hour at the most, so soon it would be over....

The doctor's brusque voice cut the air. 'I'm a bit worried Mrs Cooke. I still can't see its head. I'll have to use the drip again. I'm sorry.'

Jenny shrank back on the pillow. Francis put his arm round her. She wanted to shout out and say, 'I don't want the drip. I don't like it. It hurts.' But she didn't. She set her face into a blank mask and let them attach her to the drip again.

This time the black midwife had gone. Two young pupil midwives came instead. They were kind and held her hands, but suddenly, as one pain shot hard on the heels of another, she knew that they didn't understand. They couldn't. The hands of the clock crept up to nine o'clock. Then to half past nine.

The doctor rushed in. He said, 'I'm sorry, Mrs Cooke, but we'll have to increase the dose on the drip. I'm sorry.'

She began to bite her lip as the pains leaped upon her. She tried to breathe from the gas and air machine but the sweet, gassy smell left her dazed. The pain bit as hard as ever, anyway. Suddenly she flung the gas and air machine away from her so hard that it crashed to the floor. The midwife stifled a cry and bent to pick it up.

'Oh take it away!' said the doctor. 'She's had too much of it anyway.'

Then, hardly aware any more of what she was doing, Jenny grabbed the drip needle and pulled it out of her arm. One nurse held her down firmly, while the other slid the needle back in again. As the next pain gathered she threshed about on the bed. She clung on to Francis. But it made no difference. And still she didn't make any sound. Her mind became very clear as the effect of the drugs wore off. 'How can this be happening to me?' she thought. 'I never knew such pain existed in this world.' Two other doctors banged through the door and she heard them whispering together: 'I can't see the head. I can't see the head.' Their words tolled in her brain. No head. That meant it would never be born. Never. Never. The pain came again.

The whispering went on. 'She's strong. She'll have to wait. Wait. Yes, wait. Try not to do a Caesarean.'

The older doctors went out. The young doctor leaned against the delivery bed, his face white and lines tense round his mouth. 'She can't wait much longer,' he said. Jenny looked helplessly at the clock. It was just after ten at night. The pain came again. Her razor-sharp mind told her that it felt as if a giant had got hold of her head in one hand and her feet with the other and was slowly and inexorably bringing them together. While all her bones scrunched in the middle. In her middle. She moaned. Francis leaped up, 'Can't you do something?' he cried.

The door banged. It was quarter past ten. 'Oh God, please help me,' said Jenny wordlessly. But the next pain was worse than ever. The door banged again and in came the three doctors. There was a moment's silence. Then, 'I can't see the head. I'm worried. You'd better do a forceps.'

And now she endured the sight of the silver instruments being handled. Her legs were hung in stirrups let down from the ceiling. There was the sound of cutting. She closed her eyes and clung on to the bed. Somehow she had to hang on. Hang on. And still no cry came from her lips. The pains went on. And on. And on. It was half past ten.

Somebody said, 'Poor kid!'

She became aware that Francis wasn't there any more. The two young nurses stood one on each side of her, hardly speaking, their faces set with tiredness.

All at once the doctor cried out. 'The head! The head's being born, Mrs Cooke!'

She opened her eyes dully. How could it be when she hadn't felt the forceps yet? She turned her head away and shut her eyes.

'Mrs Cooke! Wake up! Your baby's being born.'

She opened her eyes. The doctor was holding up something a dull green colour. It made no sound. No movement. Something with a long, twisting cord.

'Don't you want to know what you've got?'

She turned her head away.

There was a silence. Then, 'It's a boy! A boy!'

It doesn't cry, she thought. It's dead. Dead. Then the thin, reedy cry battered her eardrums. She opened her eyes again. It's arms moved feebly. So it wasn't dead.

'Do you want to hold your baby?'

She found her mouth wouldn't open to say yes.

She tried to lift up her arms to welcome the child. But her arms didn't seem to work either. The nurse bustled up and put the baby in her arms. Jenny tried to clasp him, but her hands wouldn't move. So the baby had to lie on the bed next to her. She stared at its white, puckered face and closed eyes. Then she turned away and tears began to slide down her cheeks.

Later another doctor came to sew her up. When she tried to open her mouth to tell him she needed a pain-killing injection her mouth didn't work. So she endured the stitching without one. At last it was over. She stared at the clock. It was midnight. Francis went home, his face white and his eyes distraught. The nurses went. The doctor went.

Then she lay, quite alone. Two porters came in and put her on a trolley. They wheeled her down corridor after corridor. As the trolley glided along something at the very bottom of her heart began to feel warm. She remembered reading about people who tried for years and years to have a son. And failed. Some people never, ever had sons, while she, plain, ordinary Jenny, had got a son first time round. In the core of her being joy flickered. Her arms seemed to work now and she wished she could cuddle her baby but he wasn't there. They wheeled her to the ward and deftly put her to bed. They left her to fall asleep. And still no sound had left her lips.

When she woke next morning she wondered for a second why her body no longer felt heavy. Then she remembered. The baby had come early. Suddenly she bit her lip hard. Every detail of that awful night rushed into her mind. She saw her Bible on the bedside table and put her hand out for it. Then she stopped. Instead she tried to pray. But there was nothing to say. Nothing.

A nurse opened her door with a cheery laugh and gave her breakfast on a tray. Jenny arranged her face into a carefree grin. 'All right ducks?' asked the nurse.

'Fine,' lied Jenny.

She ate her breakfast slowly, all the time wondering where her baby was.

The door banged again and the sister came in with the young doctor of the night before. He looked whiter than ever. The sister said, 'We've been worried about you. How do you feel?'

'Fine.'

The sister looked searchingly at Jenny but just then the emergency light flashed on the wall and she rushed out. The doctor stood by the bed. After a moment he looked at Jenny and then looked away. 'I'm sorry, Mrs Cooke,' he said at last. 'I don't know how it happened. I'm so sorry. But you were so brave. You ought to hear some of them: screaming and swearing and throwing themselves up to the ceiling. All about nothing at all. But you....'

Jenny said nothing. She wanted to say, 'I wasn't brave. But my mouth wouldn't work. I wished I could have screamed.' Instead she said, 'Oh, it wasn't too bad.'

He looked suddenly young again. 'Are you sure? Well, that's a relief. I don't know what happened. The head must have got stuck.' He gathered up his notes and stared at her doubtfully. 'Well, if you're sure you're all right?'

'Yes,' she said quickly.

He stopped at the door and looked at her again, his eyes rimmed with weariness. 'I'm sorry,' he said. Then, 'I'll get them to send the baby down.' They looked at each other for a moment. 'I'm sorry,' he said and was gone.

When he had gone she found her shoulders were so tense that they hurt. She tried to relax and drink her coffee. Why hadn't she told them the truth? She simply didn't know. Then another nurse brought in the baby in a see-through plastic crib. She picked him up and gave him to Jenny. 'Isn't he sweet?' she said and Jenny nodded.

When the room was quiet again she held the baby in her arms. He stirred and nestled down and she felt his warmth. She examined his head. It was very round, with a down of hair and a tiny pulse beating on top. After a moment he opened his eyes. They gazed vacantly into mid-air. She bent forward and looked right into them. They were a curious navy blue colour. 'My son,' she thought. 'Jonathan.'

When she and Francis had picked this name before he was born they had been thrilled to find out it meant—'a gift from

God'. Now she frowned. A gift from God? Yes, the baby was, poor little child. But what about the pain of getting him? Was that too a gift from God? Her eyes blurred and she tried to forget.

Later Francis came, burdened down with flowers and chocolates and biscuits. He chuckled over the baby and nursed him. Then he put him back in his crib. He took her hand. 'Jenny,' he said and his face suddenly looked old.

She opened her mouth, then closed it again and shook her head. 'I can't face it again,' she whispered. He held her for a long time and said at last, 'I'm telling you, Jenny, I made up my mind last night. When they wouldn't let me stay in that delivery room. I was pacing up and down and had a row with one of those stuck-up nurses!'

A ghost of a grin hovered on Jenny's face. Same old Francis!

'When they finally let me in I was so shocked.'

'Why?' She was interested in spite of herself.

He paused. 'The whole floor was covered with blood. And you looked like no one should ever have to look like.'

He paused again.

She waited. She knew him. If he'd made his mind up about something, he was immovable.

'You're not having any more. I'll never ask it of you. Never. The only reason you'll ever have another baby, is if *you* want it. I shall never mention it again.' The tension in her shoulders snapped and she lay back on the pillows.

'But he'll be an only one...' she said 'and you ought to be able to have at least two children....'

'Nonsense. He'll be perfectly all right. And what more do I want? I've got a wife and a son.' He caressed the baby's tiny cheek. 'How many men can say as much?'

Relief flooded her. But there was something else. Something.

'All right then,' she said, but there was no joy in her reply. Only the first, faint flutter of fear.

CHAPTER FOURTEEN

I SIMPLY DON'T UNDERSTAND IT!

Confused, I stumbled endlessly
uphill. Had to fight fearsome
 things
as big as ogres. Ford the black
 river
within. Was weighted down with
 pain.
Heard no answer to my call.
Which made the dark seem
 darker....

Jenny Cooke, 1978

On the eighth day after the birth Jenny lay back in their bed at home. Jonathan was asleep for once. After a moment she crawled out of bed and slumped down in a kneeling position. Her mind ached with a question. Other people had miraculous answers to prayer. They had healings. They gave marvellous testimonies. She'd seen them and heard them. But what had she got? She buried her head in the bedspread. She'd got nothing. When her whole being had cried out to God on that delivery bed, there had been no help.

She stretched out her arms across the bed. It was no use flying into a rage anyway. She'd learned that at the Deaf School. But this? This was worse than anything else that had happened to her in all her life before. Her tears slid on to the covers and she blew her nose.

'Lord,' she said at last. 'If you want to tell me, please will you tell why. I'd like to know why.'

The room was quiet. She picked herself up and crept back to bed. They'd prayed so much beforehand. They'd trusted. They'd believed.

She picked up the Bible and opened it at random. Her eyes read,

> For we know that up to the present time
> all of creation groans with pain,
> like the pain of childbirth.
> But it is not just creation alone which groans;
> we who have the Spirit as the first of God's gifts
> also groan within ourselves, as we wait for God
> to make us his sons and set our whole being free.[1]

[1] Romans 8:22–23 (Good News Bible)

She frowned, shut the Bible and then opened it again. She reread the words. How strange that she had never noticed them before. So Paul said he groaned within himself, waiting.... How did that fit in with the triumphant cry she'd so often heard at meetings: 'With his stripes we are healed!'[1] She pushed the book away. It was too much. She didn't understand. Yet her mind was comforted.

But later, in the middle of the night, when the baby had screamed for over two hours and nothing pacified him, when she leaped out of bed for the umpteenth time and her knees gave way so that she fell to the floor and had to claw her way back up, she was amazed to hear her own raucous voice yelling out at the baby, 'You hurt me! You hurt me!'

She found herself shaking his carrycot with one hand while the other was clenched into a fist. Suddenly Francis was at her side. He led her away and tucked her up in bed. Then he nursed the baby. She lay, wide awake, her body aching and her mind a bruise. Why? she asked again. Then she thought about the girls who had no husband or a husband who was away or didn't care. Who helped those girls in the night? There was no answer to that.

Slowly she got stronger. The baby thrived and they settled down as a family. As long as she felt well, the house was tidy and the baby quiet, she knew she could cope. But once any one of those things broke down, she broke down too. She loved the baby but often found herself unaccountably shouting at him. He gazed back, without understanding, his brown eyes puzzled and watchful.

If only somebody would help me,' she cried to herself. But day after day slipped by. No one phoned. No one came. No one helped.

'All those church meetings I used to go to,' she said to Francis one night. 'No one bothers with me now. It's as if I don't exist.' She flung her magazine down and stormed into the kitchen.

'Don't be too hard on them, Jenny,' he said, following her. 'They've got their problems too, I expect.'

'Well, after all that spouting on about love and caring!

[1] Isaiah 53:5

When it comes to the crunch, who helps me? Who cares?'

'I do.'

She hung her head for a minute and there was silence. Then she lifted it again. 'Sorry,' she said in a small voice. 'I didn't mean you. And there's my mum who comes such a long way to see me every week. And your mum. And my aunts and Sue.' She sighed. 'I always do make my mind up a bit too hastily, don't I?'

He smiled and said nothing.

'And,' she said, 'there's a few friends in the road...' her voice trailed away. She turned back to the sink and began to peel potatoes.

One evening a few days later she began to tell him about the night Jonathan was born. All at once she stopped. 'I told you this last night, didn't I?'

He nodded.

She stared at him. 'I tell you it every night, don't I?'

He nodded and moved closer to her.

'I don't know why I do it. I sort of have to. It's strange. My mum's the same. Every now and then out comes the story of the day I was born.'

He said, 'I don't mind.'

'But aren't you bored?'

'No.'

'It's as if I've got to relive it. Get it out of my system. It won't...go away.'

He sat in the quietness of the room. If he was worried he never showed it.

'I've no one else to tell but you. And there's another thing.'

'Mmmm?'

'I keep shouting at Jonathan. I...I....' She shuddered.

He sat up very still and alert.

She said, 'I can't cope with him. I do love him, only sometimes...well, quite often really, I wish he weren't there. No that's wrong. I wish I didn't have to look after him. I'm so hopeless at this mothering business. I've *never* been interested in babies like some girls are. Oh, I wish I could rest. And forget. Just sleep and sleep and sleep.'

Francis said nothing.

She thought about the daily yelling matches between her-

CHAPTER SIXTEEN

THE NIGHT CHOICE

At last, despairing, raised my eyes
and saw
the rocky way irradiated, bright
with reflected light. Then I knew
that
you are older than all darkness
And more kind.

Jenny Cooke, 1978

It was just before Jonathan's first birthday, when Jenny spoke up to Francis one evening. 'You know, I've been thinking a lot about whether to have another child.'

He watched her carefully.

'I think I now feel it would be the best way for us as a family. Only, Francis....'

'Mmm.'

'I'm scared. I'm... terrified.' She sat, hunched on the edge of her chair, her shoulders tense, her face drawn. 'And there's no one I can tell. Only you.'

'Are you sure? I mean really sure?'

She closed her eyes. She wanted to say, 'If I refuse to have another child, it'll be because of fear. And the more I'm afraid, the bigger the fear gets. It's like a Goliath. It fills all my mind.'

Instead she lifted up her chin and said, 'For some daft reason I refuse to give in.' Her hands clenched and unclenched. 'I've got to face it. I can't live in fear for the rest of my life.'

Francis was silent for a long time. At last he said, 'Oh, Jenny, I never thought you'd say a thing like that!'

'Why not?'

'Well, it's, er, not like you.'

She flushed. 'It *is* like me. I've never given in. Well, nearly never anyway.'

He said, 'Look, I didn't mean to say this now, only I've got to. I'm a bit fed up of being like a father to you. And you clinging on. Never even making a phone call without me being there. I love you. And I want you to be my equal. Not a sort of young wife!'

'Well really! What a cheek!'

They stared at each other angrily, across the lounge, all the baby talk forgotten.

'And I,' she said crisply, 'am sick of being your little pet. Pampered and fussed till I could scream. I want... I want....'

'To grow up?'

She tossed her head. 'Hmmph! Well, if I'm trying to catch you up, don't get to the grandfather stage too quickly, will you!' Then she ducked suddenly as a cushion sailed across the room.

They stared at each other for some moments and then, quite suddenly, both began to laugh.

It was while they were on holiday in Cornwall that Jenny became pretty certain she was pregnant again. It made her feel important and she hugged the secret to themselves. Then one afternoon as they were driving across Bodmin Moor, the pains started in her stomach. By the time they got back to the holiday farmhouse she was weeping in agony.

Later, when all hope of any baby had gone, she pretended she didn't mind. But Francis wasn't fooled. Once they got home he called their own doctor. He was kindly, but practical. 'Try again next month,' he said and smiled heartily.

But nothing had quite prepared Jenny for the weeks that followed. Her fear was replaced by an emptiness, a barrenness that made her mourn for the lost child as if it had been known and loved. Each day seemed surrounded by a circle of darkness. The blackness pressed itself all around her. Her limbs felt heavy as if she couldn't move them. A strange weight pressed on her back. And in her mind drummed the refrain: there's no point in living. No point. No point. No point.

She couldn't pray. She couldn't read. She couldn't sleep. One evening in early summer she said to Francis, 'I wish I was dead.'

He started up and shook her hard. 'Stop it! Stop it!' he shouted. 'Don't you care for Jonathan any more?'

'Yes. But I wanted the other one.' She began to shake and sat down suddenly on the bed.

He said, 'Will you pray?'

She shook her head.

He said,'I'm telling you, you *will* pray. Now. With me!'

Obediently she sat still, as if frozen. He prayed. She made no sound. And then an idea took root in her mind. She tried to open her mouth. It clogged. Like a drowning man reaching or the last straw, she forced her mouth to open. Instead of a weak prayer slipping out, she heard her voice make a great cry. 'You evil power,' she cried. 'Get away from me! Tempting me towards death. In the name of Jesus, get off my back. Leave me alone!'

The room was startled. Then it went still. Slowly she felt her back straighten. The strange weight lifted off. The blackness dwindled. She sat on and Francis held her hand.

'Francis, am I going off my head?'

'No.' He laughed suddenly. 'You're in good company.'

'What!'

'Martin Luther used to throw his inkpot at the devil. You've just done the same!'

'Oh, Francis. I...I...feel better.' She jumped up and began to walk round the room. 'It's gone! That awful darkness has gone!'

A few weeks later she was sitting up in bed one morning and said, 'Francis, I still feel sad about losing the baby, but that awful blackness has never come back. And I've realized that the Lord is the author and giver of life. It's not us with all our cleverness and contraception and things. In the end it's him. And there's something else too. A woman down the road. She's just lost a baby. She says I'm the only person who understands. I'd never have got her confidence otherwise.'

At what a cost though, thought Jenny as Francis went down to make some tea. A great privilege to have the woman's confidence, but bought at great cost. There was far more to this being 'ordinary' than she thought.

She sat on, savouring the last few minutes in bed. Then, all at once, she became aware that the warmth of the presence of her Lord was approaching.

'Yes?' she said.

He waited and she poured all her heart out to him. Quick as lightning came the reply. 'By this time next year you will hold your baby in your arms.'

'But...?'

The immediate sense of him had gone. Only the memory remained and the memory, too, of many different women in the Bible who had been barren and who had, in the end, been promised a child. And children were born to them. She lay back on the pillows and the old peace welled up inside her.

Some weeks later she sat up, wide awake, in the middle of the night. It was so dark she could hardly see the shape of the furniture in the bedroom. What on earth had woken her up? She tried to settle down again but it was no use. She touched Francis with her toe. He slept peacefully on. She sighed and shut her eyes again. As she did so she seemed to see a picture in her mind's eye. It was like a waking dream. She turned over in the bed, irritably pulling up the sheets. 'No,' she said to herself, 'I want to go to sleep.' The picture persisted. She sat up again. 'Well?' she said at last.

She concentrated on the picture. It was of a bleak, dark mountain. There were two pathways over it. One curved through fields on the lower slopes. The other...she blinked and bit her lip. The other went straight up over the top. It was steep, barren and rutted with stones and boulders. She put up her hands to her ears. No, she said wordlessly. I don't want to.... Then came words, inner words, that sank into her mind like stones. 'You can choose which way you want to go. I know you love me and promised to follow me.'

She bowed her head.

'If you choose the easier way I will not blame you. I will bless you and give you a ministry here and now, locally.'

She waited, knowing before she heard it what the rest of the message would be: 'Or you can choose the harder way. It's the better way for you. A narrow way. If you do, you will suffer. You will dwell in total obscurity. You will be ill and have to go to hospital. If you do this for me, I will bless you. I will give you a much wider ministry many years from now. You can choose.'

She lay a long time quite still. At last she said in a whisper, 'Can I have a day...or two...to think it over? It's a big decision.' The room was very peaceful and she knew she was being granted the time.

Next morning she tried to dismiss the event, the night

choice, from her mind. Perhaps it was all her imagination. It wasn't scriptural in content. She'd made a mistake. Eaten curry for supper. But, as the day wore on, a story she wished she hadn't heard came strongly to mind. She remembered the Israelites, called out of Egypt, led by Moses, crossing the Red Sea, into the wilderness. Then a choice of ways was presented to them. And they didn't have the faith. So they were left wandering for forty years, ever in sight of the Promised Land, but never entering, never finding what God wanted for them in *this* life.

A couple of evenings later, casually, as she walked upstairs to give Jonathan a hot drink, she said, 'Lord, I didn't duck out of the hard choices I had to make before, when I chose to follow you. So why should I now? Okay. I choose. It's the steep path.' Then, shoulders squared, she went into her son's bedroom.

Yet somehow in the months that followed the memory of the choice fell to the back of her mind. All was well in the family, especially when she discovered she was pregnant again. Eventually she forgot all about the night choice.

CHAPTER SEVENTEEN

'YOU AND YOUR MIND!'

One in nine of us will at some time be treated in a mental hospital. This makes it fairly likely that it will happen to one of our family or friends, if not to us....

TV Times
April 10th 1984

JENNY SAT ON the kitchen floor. All around her were piles of sheets, towels and pillowcases waiting to be washed. In the corner was a bucket of dirty nappies. The washing-up bowl was full of cold, greasy water and breakfast pots were strewn over all the kitchen working surfaces. She tried to lever herself up and make an attempt to pick up the sheets, but it felt as if weights were attached to her arms and legs, so she slumped back and put her head in her hands.

Just then Jonathan raced in the doorway. He tore past her and hurled open a cupboard. He scrabbled inside it and brought out a pile of baking tins, which he began to bang with a toy rolling pin. The din increased. She put her hands over her ears. Please be quiet, her mind begged. Nothing happened.

'Shut up!' she yelled.

He looked round, startled, dropped the rolling pin and began to cry.

Oh no! she thought. She crawled over to him and tried to cuddle him. He resisted, pushed her away and ran into the hall. She leaned her head against the pantry door. Please help me. Someone. Anyone. Please help me.

Then he was back again. He trotted up to her and held out his favourite teddy. She took it and pressed it against her cheek. He stared at her, his eyes puzzled, and then came and nestled up to her.

'Biscuit?' he said. She ruffled his hair. He was sweet... but if only she didn't feel so sick, so weak, so tired.

Next morning she was worse than ever, so Francis got the doctor. He came into the bedroom, peered at her and then lifted the phone. 'I've got a seriously ill patient here!' His voice boomed. 'She's got to be admitted at once!'

When she was finally settled into St Mary's in a room next to the sister's office, the registrar came and examined her. She recognized him as the older doctor who had been with her when Jonathan was born. After a while he sent out the nurses and came and sat by her. He picked up her New Testament from the locker. 'Are you a Christian?' he asked.

She nodded.

'So am I.' There was a pause. 'Now tell me what's really the matter!'

She opened her mouth.

He said, 'You had all the symptoms of acute appendicitis when you came in, which is not the ideal illness to have when you're four months pregnant. You gave us all quite a fright, I can tell you.' He waited. 'All the symptoms have disappeared now. You are perfectly all right. But....'

She looked up at him.

'You're suffering from exhaustion. True exhaustion. Tell me about it.'

She bit her lip and said, her voice trembling a little, 'I'm terrified. I keep thinking I'm going off my head. I keep shouting...at my little boy...wanting to...hit him...he's....'

Her voice was so low that he had to bend forward to catch her words. Silently he passed her a paper hanky. She forced herself to look at him and saw that he was watching her intently and behind the kindness in his eyes was a sorrow. He picked up her hand, squeezed it gently and put it down again.

'You see, dear,' he said, 'it's too much for you.'

'But other girls manage.'

'Yes. But I'm not talking about other girls. I'm talking about you. You've had a toddler, a miscarriage and another pregnancy all in two and a half years. You're exhausted.' He got up from the chair. 'You're to stop blaming yourself and start getting better.'

'But?'

The Sister came in and stood at the end of the bed. 'Crisis over, doctor?'

He grinned and became official again. 'Yes. She won't

have to be rushed to theatre after all. I am prescribing complete bedrest for at least a week. Possibly a month. She's to stay in this hospital until she feels quite well.' He turned and gave Jenny one last glance. 'It's doctor's orders! As *long* as you like.' He smiled and was gone.

The time in hospital passed. She rested and ate and read magazines. She prayed. She read the Bible. She felt as if a weight had been lifted off her shoulders. The Lord had answered her desperate cry for help and she felt at peace for the first time in months.

As she rested she realized that she had been very unhappy. For years. And yet how could that be, when she had Francis and Jonathan, and loving relatives and parents, and a nice house and professional qualifications and had been filled with the Spirit and...? 'I feel as if I'm searching for something,' she thought. 'But I don't know what it is!' And the more she tried to work it out, the less she understood. And how could she ever find what she was looking for, if she didn't know what it was? She sighed and turned back to the magazines.

She read an article about women who were treated as Outpatients at Mental Hospitals. After a while the magazine slipped from her fingers. A frown creased her forehead, as she lay back and thought about the one in ten of all women who had to be treated. Could it be true? One in ten? She shuddered. She knew why now. Or, at least, half why. She had grasped what it meant to suffer in the mind. In the magazines she read other things. They were horrible things about women who went mad, or who battered their children or who even killed them. She grieved for such children. She bowed her head. After a moment she raised it again. But what had driven these women to such desperation? She stared straight ahead. For the first time in her life she realized she had the inklings of an understanding. And of a compassion for such mothers.

She watched an older, very smart staff nurse whisking round the ward. Jenny smiled to herself and then bit her lip. She thought all about the Women's Lib. talk. She could never imagine herself being a wife, and a mother, and having a fascinating profession as well, *and* being smartly dressed, not to mention being a person in her own right on top of all that. She'd never make those heights but sink back into oblivion and the ordinary struggle that made up ordinary life. She sighed and turned over in the bed. If only she knew what it was she wanted to do. There was something...something else. But she didn't know what it was. She didn't know its name. She had better be content with being ordinary.

Suddenly she sat up straight. No one was ordinary. People suffered. They suffered terribly, behind all the masks of ordinary routines and mortgages and holidays and bringing up the kids. She sighed. It was too much. Now her body felt so much better her mind seemed to be bursting.

She grinned as she saw Francis through the glass door. He rushed in and said, 'How are you?'

'Much better. Oh, Francis, I've been having so many strange ideas!'

He laughed and, all at once, looked years younger. 'You and your mind!' he said. 'Come on then. Tell me all about it. I guess I'll hear it anyway, so go on!'

One afternoon a few weeks after she came home, she began to ask herself yet again what it was she was searching for. All at once the room went intensely still.

'Your mind.' The words plopped into her thoughts like a stone into a pool.

'My mind?'

'Love the Lord your God with all your *mind*.'

'My mind!'

She sat quite still for a long time. Her mind! She'd forgotten she had a mind. She thought of all her English studies, her books, her winning the school scholarship to go to university—all forgotten for years and years. Her certificates were shoved into drawers in the back bedroom, her books gathering dust. 'But,' she stammered, 'I...I...thought if I was a good wife and mother I had to stay at home like church people say, and do as Francis says,' she suddenly grinned in spite of herself, 'and go to coffee mornings and prayer meetings and look after babies and pretend I was happy.'

The room went very quiet again. Then, 'Love the Lord your God with all your heart, with all your soul, with all your strength and with all your *mind*.'

She was silent while the truth of the ancient words sank into her. She waited. Then she said, 'If you want me to love you with my mind, then please send my mind something to do.' No doubt in a year or two God would answer.

A couple of days later she had put Jonathan in his bath when the phone rang. She rushed to answer it, calling out to her mother-in-law as she did so, 'Keep an eye on Jonathan for me will you? He's in the bath.' She picked up the receiver. 'Hello?'

A beautifully southern English accent replied, 'Is that Jenny Cooke?'

'Yes?'

'My name's Michael Harper.'

Several thoughts flashed through her mind all at once. Could it be *the* Michael Harper, one of the most well-known Christians in the country, who led all the charismatic meetings and ran *Renewal* magazine and sent it all over the world? She'd seen him at big rallies and heard him preach about the baptism in the Holy Spirit and now thousands of people up and down the land in the Anglican Church had been blessed. Only all the meetings and houseparties were too far away; she and Francis could never afford to go and nothing ever happened in the North and...she pulled herself together.

'Er, yes,' she said and her voice came out squeaky.

He began again. 'You wrote to me recently at *Renewal* magazine.'

'Did I?'

'In response to an article on the poor. You wrote about a group of children you have in your house. With a dog!' He chuckled.

'Oh yes. I remember now.'

He said, 'It was a super letter. You can write well. Will you make it into an article for us?'

'An article?'

'Yes. About seven hundred words.'

She stared at the phone. 'But I'm no good. I mean won't people think we're setting ourselves up...oh, dear, I don't know what I mean. But,' she struggled on, 'you see, it's only ordinary. Not exciting. Not lots of conversions, like you usually read about in Christian books.'

There was a pause. The phone crackled. He said quietly, 'But that's the whole point. Most Christians feel so defeated anyway, that they feel even worse when they read these triumphalist books. But if you write an article like your letter, they could relate to that.'

'Oh.' All at once her chest felt warm. 'Do you really think so?'

'Yes. Will you do it?'

'Yes. Yes, I will. Thank you very much.'

She put the phone down and stared, dazed, round the bedroom. She clasped her hands round her knees and began to think. The unborn baby kicked her and she stood up quickly. The article had better be written before July or else it would never get done. In a dream she went to the bathroom. Her mother-in-law was sitting by the bath with a pair of scissors in her hand. 'Jenny, I'm terribly sorry, only he did it before I got in here!'

Jenny gazed at the bath water and then at Jonathan. She looked at her mother-in-law and they both began to giggle helplessly. Jonathan turned and joined in the laughter, his shorn head wagging from side to side, while all around him his brown hair floated in the bath water.

It was only after she'd written the article and posted it that the understanding came to her. She had enjoyed writing it. She suddenly remembered other things from long ago: wanting to be a writer and always reading and listening to plays on the radio, and sitting by the canal at school reading poetry. Always it was words. Words made her happy. I was happy when I wrote that article, she thought. For the first time in years I was truly happy! Hadn't the Lord once intimated to her, 'One day you will write....' But under the weight of all the years and years of teaching and babies she'd forgotten. For seven years she had been unhappy. Always searching. Never finding. Because she had forgotten she loved words. She sat on. So that was why the Lord had not answered her prayers for peace and joy. If he had she would never have discovered again that she loved words. And seemingly he had given her the love for words in the first place.

But words were not going to be enough to help her through the next childbirth. She pushed away the folder with the copy of the article in it and prayed again, as she had done every day now for several months. 'Lord, please forgive me, only I'm terrified of having this baby. Please help me.'

She read a passage from Hebrews 11. Some people there did great and mighty deeds and saw miracles by their faith. And others, she sighed. Others, equally by faith, suffered greatly. She sighed again. What little faith she had simply consisted of believing God heard her. And that was all.

It was very early one June morning when she woke Francis up. 'I've been getting pains,' she said.

They did all they had to do and then went to hospital. She tried to relax. She knew what she was going to face. Only last week one doctor had said brusquely to her timid question. 'No, second births aren't always easier. Sometimes they are much worse.'

She lay in the labour room. It was just the same. The drip attached to her arm, a pethidine injection making her float away, Francis looking worried. She looked at the clock. It was half past two in the afternoon. It was then that she heard the inner voice, so quiet, so gentle that it was scarcely audible. 'You'll have six much harder contractions.'

She endured them. Yes, there were six.

Then the voice came again. 'You'll have three terrible ones.' There was no time for her to debate whether this was God's voice. She clung to the fact that she knew her Lord and believed him.

A midwife shot in. 'You'll have about three very difficult contractions now,' she yelled. 'Hang on, love.'

Jenny panted and sobbed her way through the three.

The inner voice said, 'Only one now. Then that's it.'

Jenny hung on the bed.

The midwife said, 'I'm very sorry, Mrs Cooke, you've some time to wait. It's very difficult for you, it's....' Suddenly her voice stopped. Then, in a tone of wonder, she said, 'I'm wrong. You're ready for delivery now. How extraordinary.' They rushed her down the corridor.

'Quick,' yelled the midwife.

They propped her up on pillows.

'You'll push eight times,' said the inner voice.

Jenny forgot everything: the inner voice, Francis, everything. She pushed. The pains came, but they didn't hurt. She felt them, but they didn't hurt. She could feel the baby, like a round ball, a world in itself, sliding down through her body. It seemed like a few seconds, before someone said, 'The head's coming!'

Then voices started shouting, 'Get oxygen! Oxygen!'

She heard a voice, as if from a great distance, 'Look, Mrs Cooke! Look!'

She looked. A tiny, black-faced baby was being rushed past her. The midwife held Jenny's hand. 'It's a girl!' Then, 'Don't worry. She was strangling in the cord, but we cut it. She'll be all right. Yes, there she goes.' The baby's cry flooded the room.

'Why's her face black?' Jenny tried to ask, but already they were putting the baby into her arms, the tiny, blue face flushing pink.

'She's all right,' said the midwife. 'Thank God.'

'I do thank God,' whispered Jenny.

The baby was pinker than ever now and breathing normally. Suddenly Jenny caught sight of Francis' face under the cap and mask. His eyes were one enormous smile. He came to her and they gazed at each other.

'A girl,' she said. 'Deborah. We've got a girl.'

He nodded. They didn't need to say any more. The air between them was full of all the unspoken words of love.

Later as she lay back in the ward, the baby asleep on her breast, joy swept over her. The birth had been so quick, only taking forty minutes from the six hard contractions. The agonizing bit had only lasted five minutes! She read from her Bible, 'My soul doth magnify the Lord, And my spirit hath rejoiced in God my Saviour. For he hath regarded the low estate of his handmaiden.'[1]

She lay back, spent and joyous. After all the fear, all the screwing up of courage, she had been rewarded in a special way. A special grace for a special labour.

[1] Luke 1:46–48

Later Francis said, 'The midwife said she had never seen a birth like yours in all her experience. She said she was amazed.'

Jenny smiled peacefully. 'No wonder she was amazed. I was amazed myself!'

When he had gone she repeated the precious words: 'My soul doth magnify the Lord, And my spirit hath rejoiced in God my Saviour.'

CHAPTER EIGHTEEN

MUMMY! MUMMY!

About this time the state and happiness of these poor people at Bedford was thus, in a dream or vision, represented to me. I saw, as if they were set on the sunny side of some high mountain, there refreshing themselves with the pleasant beams of the sun, while I was shivering and shrinking in the cold, afflicted with frost and snow and dark clouds.

Methought, also, betwixt me and them, I saw a wall that did compass about this mountain; now through this wall my soul did greatly desire to pass....

Grace Abounding
John Bunyan

A FEW WEEKS after they had moved to a new house, Jenny was talking to Helen, her new next-door neighbour. Helen poured Jenny a cup of tea in a china cup and then said, all of a sudden, 'What do you think will happen when the world ends?'

'...pardon?'

'You know. It's in the Bible. When Jesus comes back.' There was a pause. Helen looked at Jenny. 'I wish I could study the Bible,' she said.

Jenny stared, open-mouthed. 'Er...yes,' she said, weakly.

The next day a friend telephoned. 'There's a lonely Christian living near you. Do you know of any Bible Study groups nearby?'

'I'm not sure,' said Jenny.

That afternoon she went out to tea and met the cousin of another neighbour. Hazel leaned forward over her piece of chocolate cake and said suddenly, 'Do you go to church?'

'Yes.'

'I wish I could study the Bible!'

Jenny's eyes shone. 'It's funny,' she said quickly, 'this week people have kept saying that to me. I'll see if I can arrange something.'

The following day Jenny went round to another neighbour's house. She knocked on the door. Pam opened it. Jenny swallowed.

'Er, Pam, if we had a Bible Study, would you like to come?'

Pam looked blank a minute and then her face cleared. 'Yes. Why not! Will it matter that I'm a Catholic?'

'Course not!'

Pam grinned and said, 'Do you remember the first time you came round? After I told you I felt so awful after my third child was born?'

Jenny nodded. She had gone round, her feet strangely slow, while the inner voice of conscience said urgently, 'Go and see Pam. Go and see Pam. Go and see Pam.'

Pam had said, 'I feel I can't go on.'

Jenny said all in a rush, 'I used to feel like that. And I well, I prayed, and God helped me.'

There was a silence. Then Pam said, 'It's strange you should come round and say that. How strange. I'd lost my faith for years and last night I felt so bad, I prayed for the first time for years and years. I said, if there's a God, help me. Help me.'

Now there was a pause between the two women.

'I'll come to your study,' said Pam.

The group flourished. Several neighbours joined in. Some weeks up to twenty women came with droves of children. They met in each others' houses. They had evening meetings when husbands came as well and Francis took the chair.

Jenny's days were filled to bursting with the children, arrangements for the meetings, visiting those who were ill and generally helping out.

Daphne Graham became the co-leader and was a tower of strength. Sometimes they held Arts and Crafts exhibition mornings and new neighbours came along and everyone brought something they had made: pottery, tapestry, paintings, poems, dresses and basket work. And at the end someone spoke about what it meant to be a Christian. Sometimes they had candlelit evenings with poems, songs and carols and again at the end a word about the meaning of Christmas or Easter.

Jenny was amazed as she watched the twenty to thirty or so different people coming in through her front door. They were people who didn't usually go to church: men from the evening classes she went to, husbands and friends, and friends of friends. They all piled in. She remembered how in their old house she and Francis had prayed for five years to be able to talk about their faith to the people who had lived in their road. And the opportunities had been few and far between. Now they had moved, it was as if the opportunities came without being asked for. She looked round the circle of intent faces. She guessed that most people were interested in God and the meaning of life. It was just the Church they weren't interested in. She sighed.

The following day she found herself thinking about the Church again. The local church was big and growing bigger. It was said to be one of the most thriving in the North-West. There were over three hundred teenagers in the Youth Club alone. The vicar was kind and immensely strong. So perhaps they did not need the pentecostal experience. After all, the church thrived on the simple evangelical message.

So why did she pray for renewal to break out there? Who did she think she was anyway? Perhaps she was wrong. Perhaps the Holy Spirit really didn't work any more as he had done in Acts. She climbed slowly up the stairs and went into their bedroom. She thought for some time.

But then she raised her head. And she thought again. Could she really go back on what the Lord had done in her life? Could she pretend the immense joy of the release of the Spirit in her life did not exist? Could she drop speaking in tongues in private prayer, and deny the Lord's gift? Her head fell forward on to her chest. Her integrity and her very self were at stake. In the quietness of the room she raised her chin very high. No. She would not go back on what the Lord had done. And, her head still high, she ran downstairs to prepare the evening meal.

A few days later the doorbell rang. Jenny answered it. Pam was on the doorstep and Jenny began to listen to what she was saying. At the same moment Jonathan tore up. He reached up for Jenny's face, grabbed it and twisted it round so she was facing him. She pulled away, but he twisted it again, with his rough, chapped hands. 'Let go!' she said and pushed him away.

He opened his mouth and began to talk very loudly. 'Look at me!' he shouted. 'Look at me!'

Jenny got Pam inside and tried to speak to her but Jonathan thrust himself between them again. The more Jenny talked the louder he yelled, until she could neither hear herself nor Pam. At last Jenny gave in. 'What do you want?'

she asked.

His face was bright red. 'Talk to *me*!' he yelled.

'Don't be silly,' she said and pushed him away.

When the evening came the memory of the scene came back to her, unbidden.

'That child of yours gets worse and worse,' she said irritably to Francis. 'I really can't stand him at times. Whereas Debbie now, she's so sweet and good.' Francis looked at her silently. His face was weary, but she didn't notice. 'I can't wait till he goes to school,' she said, 'and then I can get some peace.' Another memory came, but she squashed it at once, without looking at Francis. The remembrance persisted: a friend saying, 'Haven't you got a super boy!' And she had wondered for a second who the super boy was. There must be a mistake. The only boy she knew was strident and he kicked.

'Super boy?' she repeated dully. 'Oh. Oh, I see. Yes. I suppose so.'

The first day he went to school, she came home and waited for the peace to come. Instead her heart ached in an unusual way. She couldn't understand it. On the fifth day he suddenly lay down in the school corridor and screamed and sobbed. 'Mummy!' he cried. 'Mummy! Mummy!' She turned and walked away, pressing her hands to her ears. The memory of his cries haunted her all day.

At the first Parents' Evening the headmistress said, 'I'm very sorry, Mrs Cooke, but Jonathan, er...rolls on the floor all day. He doesn't seem to want to learn. All the others can read now.'

Jenny went scarlet. When she got home she burst into his room and shook him hard. 'You stupid boy!' she shouted. 'Fancy letting me down like that!'

He began to yodel like a red indian. A great tide of rage welled up in her. 'I wish I'd never had you!' she said and stormed out, slamming the door.

Afterwards she couldn't settle down in the kitchen. She paced up and down. She glanced at Francis. He was reading. She clenched her hands hard at the sink. Then she turned and trailed upstairs. She went to Jonathan's room. He was still awake. She sat by his bed. 'I, Jonathan...?'

He looked at her, his eyes watchful.

'I'm sorry. I do love you really. I *am* glad I had you.' She forced herself to put the words into a prayer with him. Afterwards she looked at him helplessly. The poor thing obviously couldn't help not being able to read. Perhaps he wasn't very bright. He moved up so she could sit closer to him. 'I don't know why I get so mad with you,' she said.

One night she had a dream. She dreamed she went to the school to meet him. When she got there she saw a child's painting of a cherry tree on the front door of the school. She went up close and saw, with a shock, that Jonathan's name was on it. It must be a mistake she thought in the dream. His paintings are hopeless.

A couple of nights later she had another dream. This time Jonathan was pulling her into the school and hustling her down the corridor. They came to an oak chest. He opened the lid. Inside were sheets and sheets of beautifully neat written work and carefully coloured drawings. She glanced at them and then looked away. He said, 'Look at them, Mummy. Look at them! *Look*!' So, in the dream, she looked. Each one had his name on. 'You've done these! You?' she said.

He nodded.

'Rubbish! You can't even read!' He flinched. 'But look, Mum!'

She woke up. After breakfast she trailed round the house. It was no good. The problem of Jonathan was becoming insistent. Everything about her life was good. Except him.

That evening she said to Francis, 'I'm a bit worried about Jonathan.'

He put down his paper. 'I mean,' she went red, 'about *me* and Jonathan.' There was a pause. 'I'm wondering if I've got a problem....' Her voice trailed away.

Silence filled the room. Carefully he folded his paper. He got up, crossed the room and took her hand. 'Oh, Jenny,' he said very quietly, 'I've been worried about it for so long.'

It was her turn to stare, horrified. 'But, I, er....' Her voice broke off. What could she say?

Afterwards she sat with her head in her hands. She had spent so long building up the Bible Study group, making herself a success and being popular. Now it was all coming crashing down round her ears. She searched her heart about the boy. She knew she loved him. So why did she have these other destructive feelings, almost like hate? She licked her lips. Her heart said, 'I'll try and be open Lord. I'll try and work it out'...only it would be easier to forget it all and hope it would go away. It was so hard. So very hard to admit she had failed. She sat on in the dusk. She had failed utterly. What on earth could she do?

CHAPTER NINETEEN

IF YOU THINK YOU'VE GOT PROBLEMS!

'We . . . are being changed [transformed/metamorphosed] . . . from one degree of glory to another'

2 Corinthians 3:18 (RSV)

'And the secret is that Christ is in you; the hope of glory.'

Colossians 1:27

ONE DAY JENNY's mother-in-law drove her and the two children into Manchester to do some shopping. Jenny leaned against the back seat and shut her eyes. Jonathan was shouting. Debbie was struggling to get out of her arms. Jenny lay back, exhausted by them.

Suddenly she opened her eyes. She sat bolt upright. She stared out of the window. There, flashing by, was the new BBC building. 'That's it!' her mind cried. 'That's what I want to do! I want to work for the BBC. Communicate! Write books!' Silently she laughed at herself, but then craned her head round again. Wistfully she watched the building grow smaller. She wished...she wished...but she shook her head. It was no use. She couldn't imagine herself ever having the time or energy to do anything like that; not to mention having the courage to open her mouth and talk to writers and media people. Who'd look at her anyway? Safe fawn coat, two children, stay at home all day: a suburban housewife with an impossible dream. She had overheard some church gossip about herself one day. 'Negative', they had called her. Well, perhaps it was true. Wearily she climbed out of the car. She looked at her mother-in-law who said suddenly, 'Come on, Jenny, I'll buy you a new blouse.'

Jenny flushed a little and then a smile lit up her face. 'Why, thank you,' she said. 'Thank you very much.'

All too soon her mother-in-law had to go home. And her own mother who came every Monday to help and talk, had to get back to her own home to make the evening meal for her father. So still the desert of the week faced her. And Jonathan. Jonathan! Yelling, hurling, full-of-life Jonathan! Even though he was at school five days a week, his presence filled her life so much that all she ever said was, 'Go away! Go away! Go away!'

One morning, while Debbie suddenly and unusually slept, Jenny switched on her radio. It was a programme called, 'If you think you've got problems!' She listened, while idly running her fingers over her bedspread. All at once her fingers stopped. They drummed for a moment. Then they clenched. She sprang up, grabbed the radio and turned it off. She tossed her head and tried to leave the room. By the door her feet stopped. She turned back and faced the blankness of the bedroom. Her finger inched back to the switch. She clicked it. The announcer's voice said, 'So you have a problem with your sixteen year old son?'

A woman answered, 'Yes. He's awful!'

Jenny sat, as if frozen to the bed. Her hands climbed up her sides and she clamped them over her ears. She couldn't listen. She couldn't.

Slowly she unclamped them again.

The announcer was saying, 'Do you like your son?'

The woman said in a small voice, 'No.'

'Do you believe in your son?'

A long pause. Then, 'No.'

Jenny flung the radio across the bed. It crackled and she turned it off. She sat on and on. Strangely no one rang up. Debbie didn't awaken. Still Jenny sat. She knew that if she got up and left the room now, her problem with Jonathan would always be with her. She knew she had to face it now. Now.

'But I don't want to,' she muttered. It was a feeble excuse and she knew it.

She half slumped to her knees. 'Lord,' she said, 'I....'

It seemed as if a weight were attached to her tongue. Words clogged. How could she tell him? Yet he knew already. Only she knew she had to tell him aloud. She knew in her bones that it was the only way.

She tried again, 'Lord, when I heard that announcer saying to that woman, "Do you like your son? Do you believe in him," I....'

The weight got worse. It seemed to press on her back and

crush her. She tried to fight it off but it wouldn't go.

'Lord, I....'

She forced her lips apart. She had to speak, whatever the cost. 'Lord, I felt as if those words were being asked of me. And as if I was replying, "No! No! No!"' She buried her head in her hands. 'Forgive me, Lord. For I have sinned. I have said cruel things to the child.' She repeated every phrase she could remember having taunted him with.

All at once the weight began to shift. It was ever so slightly at first, and then more and more, until, slowly her back straightened, she got up from her knees and stood tall in the room.

'Lord, change me. Deliver me.' The words hardly seemed necessary any more. She knew she was being heard.

Yet when Jonathan came home from school that afternoon, he seemed the same.

Later on that week, as she rounded the corner of the school road and trailed up to the gate, she caught sight of a large piece of paper on the school door. That was strange. They didn't normally pin things there. The knot of mothers moved away and she went closer to see. As she got nearer her feet suddenly stopped. She stared at the paper. It was a child's painting of a great cherry tree, festooned with pink splodges for flowers. The memory of her dream flooded into her mind. In a daze she went right up to the door. As it had been in the dream so it was in reality. Jonathan's name was written on the paper.

Then he came tearing out of the school, shirt undone, knees muddy. She grabbed his hand and dragged him to a quiet part of the playground. 'Did you do that painting on the door? Or was it another Jonathan?'

'It was me,' he said, his face frowning.

She put her arm round him. 'It's lovely. It's beautiful. Well done. Good boy!'

Suddenly he flung her away. He tore round and round the playground, whooping and yelling in delight. Then he tumbled back to her again and grinned up at her. She found herself smiling and ruffling his hair.

That evening she heard him yodelling on his tractor outside the back door. Suddenly he flung in the kitchen and bounded up to her. She opened her mouth to shout in her usual ice-cold voice, 'Shut the back door! Get your muddy shoes off! You stupid boy!' Something stopped the words in her mouth. The ice died. She closed her lips again. He came and stood very close to her. 'Mum,' he said.

'Yes?'

'I love you.' Then he careered out once more. She stared blindly after him, her eyes stinging. The floor was caked with mud. The chill night air poured through the door. But she didn't care.

In the weeks that followed it was as if there was a newsreel in her mind. Things she thought she had forgotten long ago were replayed: her father shouting at her; Tim at university swamping her; sneering men teachers; men church leaders accusing her; and always underneath it all, the memory of the lonely childhood and children bullying her. Then in with all that, the terrible birth: caused by a male child.

She realized at last that it was all so simple. And yet it was so complex. Men in her life had caused her pain. So she was getting her own back, hitting out at Jonathan and being a bully herself. It was so simple and yet so hidden; the roots so deep and the branches causing pain to herself and her child. Then there was evil latching on to it and using her and her bruised heart for its own destructive ends.

They were just an ordinary family, but the oldest story of mankind was being played out amongst them, as it was in every household. Once she had said, 'Have I got an evil spirit, Lord, to make me behave the way I do?'

Straight away the still, small voice had replied, 'No. It's *you*.'

The human heart was so deceitful, so desperately wicked, yet so beloved by God that he sent his only Son. Evangelicals used the formula so glibly: 'Repent and be saved. Accept Jesus Christ as your Lord and Saviour.' But not until her battle with herself about Jonathan had she realized the depth and root of sin and pain within herself. The only way to root it out was the narrow, hard way of bending her heart and knee to the God whom she had learned to call Lord.

Finally one evening in late February she asked Francis to pray with her in the dining-room. 'I've done everything I can now, Lord,' she said. 'But there's still one last knot in my heart to do with my relationship with Jonathan. I don't know what else to do. Please, untie it for me.' A faint tremor passed over her, like a tiny breath of wind. Then it was gone.

A few weeks later as she went to collect Jonathan from school, she saw the headmistress striding out purposefully through the main doors. 'Mrs Cooke,' she called. 'Can you come in a minute?'

Jenny's heart sank. Now what had he been up to? She trailed into the school.

The Head said, 'What's happened to Jonathan?'

'Er... I don't know. Has he been naughty?'

The Head laughed. 'Not this time! In fact something so extraordinary has happened, we're all talking about it in the staffroom. We wondered if you could explain it?'

Jenny racked her brains. '...No. What is it?'

'He's suddenly changed. It's so remarkable. He used to be so, er,' her eyes twinkled, 'naughty! Rolling about the floor and yelling, you know!'

Jenny shuddered.

'But now he comes in looking so bright, sits down, gets on with his work. Actually he was so behind, we thought he was, well, backward. But he's not like that at all now. He's pleasant and, I think, intelligent. It's all been buried somewhere. Can you explain it?'

Jenny felt numb. 'I don't know.'

'He suddenly changed. From one day to the next. Most remarkable.'

'When was this?'

The Head thought a minute. 'Late February,' she said at last. 'Did anything happen at home then, in the family?'

Jenny's mind went a complete blank. 'I don't know.'

It was only on the way home that she remembered. She stopped dead and Jonathan nearly fell over the pushchair. 'Why, late February was when we prayed for the final knot to be untied!' she said, her mouth breaking into a smile.

Jonathan gazed back blankly. 'What?' he said.

'It's all right dear,' she said. 'It's all right. Everything's going to be all right!' And singing to herself, they sped home, his legs running happily beside her. In the months that followed she said to Francis, 'I've realized something about myself. I know I get all worked up if the place is untidy and I shout. I blow up quickly and just as quickly blow down!'

He grinned.

'Only....'

'Yes?'

'I feel different inside. As if at the heart of things I've been changed.'

'Yes?'

'Before, I was against Jonathan, deep inside my heart. But *now*—I'm *for* him. Do you understand?'

'Yes!'

She clasped her hands. 'I didn't know being a Christian meant you got changed right from the inside out. It begins at the top layer and works down and down and down.' She went quiet for a minute. 'If you let him, that is. If you let him.'

CHAPTER TWENTY

COUNTING THE PENNIES

Now there was not far from the place where they lay, a castle called Doubting Castle, the owner whereof was Giant Despair, and it was in his grounds that they now were sleeping. [The giant]... getting up in the morning early, and walking up and down in his fields, caught Christian and Hopeful asleep in his grounds.... He asked them whence they were, and what they did there in his grounds. They told him they were pilgrims and that they had lost their way...and the giant therefore drove them before him, and put them into his castle, into a very dark dungeon, nasty and stinking to the spirit of these two men.

The Pilgrim's Progress
John Bunyan

IT WAS SOME time before Christmas, when Francis and Jenny were praying together as they usually did on Sunday evenings, that they suddenly both went quiet. Everything about the room went very still. At last, she said in a hesitant voice, 'I feel as if I've "seen" something. In my mind's eye, I mean. A sort of picture.'

'Go on.'

'It's as if I've seen the four of us as a family going along quite happily down a country lane, when, all at once the lane plunges down into a steep valley. It's so steep and so dark you can't see the bottom.' Her voice trailed away. 'It's filled with a swirling sort of darkness.'

'Go on,' he said.

'We go down with the lane. We disappear from view. But then, after a while we struggle up again on the other side and carry on as before, across a plateau of rich cornfields.'

He said into the silence, 'How strange. How extraordinary. I've seen almost the same thing.'

It was her turn to look astonished. Francis was not one to be given to fanciful ideas. 'What is it?' she said.

'I've seen us as a family too, only walking along a flat road, until we come to a copse of huge, black trees. The road goes through the middle of the copse, and we don't leave it. We are lost to view, but later we come out on the other side.' He paused. 'Those trees were very menacing.'

They looked at each other. 'What does it mean?' she said.

'I'm not sure,' he replied. 'But if it's a word from the Lord, he'll show us what it means. Otherwise, I don't think we should dwell on it. Simply bear it in mind.'

The weeks jostled along up to Christmas and in the general rush, the pictures they had seen, slipped to the back of their minds. There was nothing in their lives to worry them, so gradually they forgot that extraordinary Sunday evening. Soon Christmas came and went, and the short January days were upon them, filled with busyness and work.

One evening Francis was late and Jenny kept the meal back for him. She knew he would be tired after spending the day in London meeting the new American bosses who had taken over his old Company. 'These take-over bids!' he had joked that morning as he left. 'The new boss apparently wears a stetson!'

A little after eight o'clock she heard his key in the lock. She ran into the hall to greet him and then stopped. She stared, bewildered. He was standing stock still in the hall, leaning back slightly against the curtains. His face was grey and he looked older, shrunken somehow.

'What's happened?' she cried, rushing up to him.

He shook his head.

She grabbed his arm and shook it. 'Tell me! Tell me! What is it?'

'I'm finished,' he said.

'Finished? What do you mean?'

He dropped his briefcase, trudged down the hall, and slumped into a chair.

'I'm finished!' he said.

'But...?'

'I've got the sack. Been made redundant. That's it!'

She stared at him and then sat down very quickly next to him. 'But why! Why, when you set up the whole Furniture Division in the North? And it's working so well!'

He said, 'They want younger men. I'm just over forty. So I'm finished!'

'That's ridiculous!' She put her arm round him and they sat in silence for a few minutes. At last she said timidly, 'When will you have to leave?'

'As from now!'

'But?'

'I'll go in tomorrow and collect my stuff.'

'But aren't you supposed to go in and work your notice?'

'Hummmph! They can whistle for their notice!'

She lay awake for a long time that night, while he slept beside her, exhausted by his day. She tried to think it all out. He'd get another job. She'd economize with the housekeeping money, buy cheap margarine, and no chocolate biscuits, and... the thoughts whirled round her mind, until she too finally fell asleep.

Next morning he was back home by eleven. 'What a rumpus in the office,' he said. 'They're all furious about me leaving. It's made them worry about their jobs.'

'Oh no!'

'Mmm.' He threw the early afternoon paper on to the table. 'I'll start looking at the "Situations Vacant",' he said.

Soon he was writing off for other jobs. He went to several interviews. But gradually his shoulders lost their square look. 'It's always the same story,' he said in the end. ' "We want younger men, Mr Cooke!" ' He shrugged and spread his hands out.

Slowly the January days lengthened out into February. One morning he got an envelope from his former Company. Inside was a short letter and a cheque. They sat in silence together on the end of the bed and stared at the cheque.

'It'll get us a second-hand car,' he said. 'I'll have to have a car if I'm going to sell anything.' Then he began totting up on his fingers. 'And there'll be enough left to last us till May.'

'May!'

She did some rough calculations in her head. 'With Family Allowance and me being careful, I can make it last till August.' She was silent for a minute. 'At least there's no heating bills in the summer.'

They sat on in the quiet room. They had six months grace. Then what?

She said, 'I do wish we had a few savings.'

He shrugged. They had put everything they had into buying their house.

With an effort he said, 'Shall we pray?'

'All right.'

So they prayed together. But the words sounded flat and meaningless and fell from the ceiling down to the bed again. After a while he said, 'We've got to trust the Lord. Who else is there?'

The weeks of job hunting dragged on. He stayed in the house more and more, silently washing up and making beds. At last she said, 'Is this all we've come to? You've no fight left and I'm just a housekeeper! What about all our dreams? Our visions? Our ambitions? Everything!'

He didn't answer.

She said, 'How can you still trust God? The firm's chucked you out and it wasn't even your fault. How can you still trust God? What's he ever done for you?' She flung herself into a chair and her face was set in bitter lines. 'What's he ever done for me? It's one long pain! One long drag of child-rearing. And there's no renewal in the church! Not even a service where I feel truly at home!' She began to cry. 'Nothing's worked out. Everything we've ever done or tried to do has turned to dust!'

'Don't,' he said wearily. 'Don't start now.'

They sat in two separate corners of the room. Then, in a small voice, she said, 'Sorry.'

He got up and came over to her. He said, 'It's got nothing to do with trusting the Lord. The thing is, I've let him down. He hasn't let me down.'

'No,' she said. 'You haven't!'

He sighed. 'Don't forget,' he said, 'he died for us.'

But she was already out of her seat. She ran to the bookshelf and ran her hand over the shelf of paperbacks. 'Look at these!' she cried. 'Christian books!' She turned away from them in anger. 'They say, "Pray this and God'll do that". Everything works out for the people in them. But it's not like that in real life! Is it? Is it!'

He went to the shelf and picked out an older, more tattered book. He said, 'It's what the Bible says that counts, Jenny.'

She went quiet.

He thumbed through the pages. 'Jesus never promised anyone an easy life. And he certainly didn't get one himself.'

'No. And we certainly don't get one either!' she said tartly.

They sat on together in a desperate silence. All at once she said, in a different tone of voice, 'Francis, do you remember that time we were praying together before Christmas and we both saw the same picture in our minds' eye?'

'Oh yes,' he said. 'I'd quite forgotten it.'

They stared at each other. 'Perhaps it was some kind of warning? Or an explanation?' she said slowly.

'I don't know. It would seem so. But we must trust the Lord.'

The days brightened and bulbs began to peep through. Jenny longed for spring never to come. It brought August so much nearer. Francis stopped writing off for jobs and the only spark of the old Francis she thought she had known so well, was when he burst in one Thursday and said, 'That's *it*!'

She looked up from the ironing.

'I will *not* queue up in that dole queue again!'

She frowned. 'Oh yes, you will. Jonathan needs new shoes....'

'I will *not*!' he shouted, glared at her and stormed out.

She knew better than to go after him. Instead she went to her handbag and took out her purse. She poured the coins out on the table and counted them. Then she recounted the brown coins. Slowly she put them back.

She went to the ironing board and switched off the iron. Then she turned on the radio. 'Mass redundancies have been announced at steel works in South Wales,' she heard the newscaster say. 'Three thousand men will lose their jobs.'

She slumped on to a chair at the table and put her head in her hands. Three thousand men. Three thousand wives. Perhaps six thousand children or more. Without hope or dignity. For she knew now, that work not only gave people a decent wage, homes, holidays and fun, it gave meaning and shape to their lives. She wiped her tears away with the back of her hand. Without work men seemed lost. At least women had the home and children to give them a feeling of position and responsibility. But what about men? She took the purse out and stared at it again. 'Oh, Lord,' she cried out. 'Please, please, help me to find a job!'

The next evening Francis said, 'Are you going to your evening class tonight?'

'What's the point?'

'Oh go on! You'll enjoy it. I'll give you the bus fare.'

She smiled suddenly. 'Well, I suppose I do like going to

Harold Massingham's Poetry Workshop.'

'Course you do! And don't forget what he told you!'

She blushed. She remembered the night she had come home and told Francis what Harold had said about her poems: 'You have a passion for writing about Christ, Jenny. You must write about him. You must!' She had been so amazed and so excited. She bit her lip. Now it all seemed part of her past life, the part that had happened before Francis lost his job.

'Okay, dear,' she said. 'I'll go.'

She climbed on the bus and nodded and smiled to a lady whom she always saw on the same bus every week. All at once the lady came and sat next to her.

'Do you go to an evening class?' she asked Jenny.

'Er, yes.'

'Are you the teacher?'

Jenny was surprised. 'No. But I used to teach before I had my children.'

The lady leaned forward. 'I do hope you don't mind me saying this, only I'm a bit desperate. You see, I teach at night school and I want to give my job up. I'm writing a book and I'm finding it a bit much teaching as well. Would you like my job? I teach English as a Foreign Language to au pair girls and overseas students at Wilmslow and it's quite well paid.'

Jenny stared blankly at the lady. 'Your job? But....'

The lady stared back, her face white and lined, her knee bent under the weight of a heavy bag.

Jenny suddenly made her mind up. 'I've not done that subject before, but I'll take the job,' she said, sounding a lot more confident than she felt.

'Oh, that's marvellous!' said the lady. 'How incredible that I should meet you like this!'

Jenny opened her mouth and then said, 'I've been praying to find a job.' But the lady didn't seem to hear her.

In next to no time at all Jenny found herself employed as an Adult Education tutor for Cheshire County Council. Night after night she swotted up the work, always managing to keep one step ahead of the students. Then she began to get phone calls from friends of the students in her class asking her to do private coaching. Soon she was earning quite a bit each week, which she saved carefully for the cheap caravan holiday she was determined to give the family in the summer.

Francis, for ever slumped in his chair, watched her as she flew from one job to the next, rubbing away the weariness from her eyes. And the more she worked, the more silent he became. 'What stuff this Women's Lib. does talk,' she said one day, on her way out. 'Always on about fulfilling oneself in the world of work and being equal with men. As far as I can see, work's work, whatever you do. It's all tiring, mostly grind and I know I'm equal anyway.' It was only as she sat on the bus that she realized he hadn't replied. She bit her lip as she gazed out of the window. Sometimes she had to admit it wasn't any fun any more, being married to him. She felt as if she were being dragged down to a premature middle-age. The suburban houses slipped by in the darkness outside the windows. She gave herself a shake and lifted her chin up high. It was no good thinking like that. She had promised to stick to him at the wedding service and she'd made up her mind to keep her word. After all, he'd seen her through the worst of her problems with the childbirth and raising Jonathan. He had never once criticized her.

Next day, after breakfast the phone rang. She answered it and then put her head round the door. 'Daphne and the Bible Study girls want to have a prayer meeting and have invited me. Will you look after Debbie while I go?'

He sprang out of his chair and said, 'So that's all I am now is it? A childminder!'

'Well it's the least you could do for me! I'm tired out after teaching last night. I've got the chance of a coffee and a chat and I want to go.'

'Go then.'

She grabbed Debbie from the playpen and tucked her into her pram. She marched out of the house and slammed the door. But by the time she got to the prayer meeting her legs were creeping along. How could she have been so mean to him? He helped so much round the house.... Daphne opened the door and welcomed her.

'Oh Daphne,' cried Jenny, 'this redundancy business is spoiling everything between me and Francis. It's awful.' She blew her nose and stared hopelessly at the girls in the bright, suburban sitting-room. Daphne drew her in, Pam gave her some coffee and Lesley took Debbie on her knee.

'What can we do?' asked Jenny. 'It's hopeless. Hopeless.'

Daphne said, 'Shall we pray for you?'

Jenny stared at her knees. 'Well that's ever so kind of you, only I just can't pray. I feel too worn out and upset.'

'That's all right. You just sit quietly and we'll pray. Do you mind?'

Jenny shook her head. 'Of course not,' she said.

Afterwards, her spirit unlightened, but her heart warmed by their kindness, she set off back for home. Whatever was she going to say to Francis? And would he still be angry with her?

CHAPTER TWENTY-ONE

THE SUBURBAN ADVENTURE

Together we survey our land:
a farmstead built,
the nearby fields neatly furrowed,
faintly green.

Remember the winter toil:
the frozen hands,
clods of unyielding earth,
tenacious weeds.

Know the land at last
is broken to our will.
Tamed by an agony of work
into possibility.

So we stand quiet.
Then jerked with surprise, see
there is yet untouched land
rolling joyously to the horizon.

And beyond.

The Marriage
Jenny Cooke, 1977

As Jenny came round the corner she saw Francis waiting for her on the doorstep. Her heart lurched. Whatever was the matter with him now? He took hold of her elbow and pulled her into the house. She stared at his face. For the first time in weeks he was smiling.

'What's happened?' she asked.

'Nothing,' he said. 'Only did you pray for me this morning?'

'Well... the others did. I just sat there.' There was a pause. 'Francis, I'm sorry about this morning.'

His smile deepened. 'I'm sorry too,' he said. He strode into the dining-room and she followed. He turned to face her suddenly. 'I know what I'm going to do.'

'What?' she asked.

'I'm going to start my own business!'

'What!'

He sat down on the edge of a chair, his face no longer sad, but alight with ideas. 'I'll design my own range of Computer Room Furniture!' She stared at him, caught up with the idea, in spite of herself. 'You mean make and sell the same kind of thing you used to sell before you were made redundant?'

He sprang up and paced the room. 'Yes. That's it.'

'But isn't it against the law?'

'Course not! If I design my own range, it's a free market place.'

'Oh.' All at once she began to laugh. 'Oh, how exciting!'

'It'll be very hard work. But I'm going to try. I'm going to!'

She clasped her hands round her knees.

Suddenly he went very quiet. 'It'll mean we won't get any Social Security, Jenny.'

'So what! We haven't had any yet, anyway!'

'It means,' his brow creased, 'it means we might lose everything.'

'Everything?'

'Yes. Everything. The house. The lot might have to go.'

'But....'

'Dare you take the risk, Jenny? Will you be with me in the venture?'

'A suburban adventure,' she said, slowly.

'What?'

'Oh, nothing. Look Francis, I may as well be in it with you. What is there to lose? Anyway I'm your wife.'

'Right,' he said. They sat together on the floor, hands clasped, heads bowed and prayed a simple prayer. Then they sat in silence. Afterwards he said, 'There is one thing. Have we anything we can sell to make some extra cash?'

'I'll have a look,' she said.

'I'm going to see some colleagues in Manchester,' he said all at once. 'And see what's what.' He dashed out.

When he had gone she set off and went into every room. She stood for a long time in the lounge and looked at the Adam fire-place. She remembered Francis labouring to put it in for her four years before; knocking out bricks and struggling with the marble surround that he had bought at cost price. She gazed slowly round the room. She went and touched each object. A few were valuable. Most were not. Some were wedding presents. All had a story behind them. She swallowed. Goodbye, she said silently to each thing.

As she went from room to room she got quicker. But saying goodbye was no easier. At last she had finished. She came and sat down in the dining-room. They could sell the least useful things first, and leave the beds, table and chairs till last. Perhaps their money would last until November then. She sat on and looked at her hands. All her seven years of marriage had been spent in building up this home. Now, in one fell swoop, it was going to have to be dismantled. She bit her lip. The last thing to sell, of course, was the house. And at least they had a house to sell. But if they once began to get into debt, then the house would have to go too.

She sat on and waited to be enveloped with grief and

racked with sobs. Nothing happened. Idiot! she said to herself at last. She closed her eyes. She seemed to see all their possessions piled up around her. They had never really 'owned' them anyway. The Lord had lent them to her and Francis to use and enjoy. So if he wanted them back.... A lightness seeped into her. All the weight of the possessions and caring for them drifted away. 'I don't understand it,' she thought, 'but if we sell them all, I won't mind, deep down.' Oh, yes, she'd be upset, but, to her amazement, at the heart of things, she knew it didn't matter. And with a strangely joyful heart she got up to prepare their tea.

And so began a time of work, such as neither of them had ever known before. Francis worked from morning till night in the garage, hammering, sawing, measuring. Then sometimes he rushed up to the back bedroom and worked on designs and advertising material. Slowly, ever so slowly, a range of Computer Room desks began to emerge. Jenny lived in a haze of exhaustion, riding miles on buses to do coaching work with shy Arabs, always with the good-natured Debbie in tow. Sometimes when she got off the bus after ten at night and found the washing-up still not done, the children not in bed and the place a mess, she would sit on the settee with tears sliding down her cheeks. Francis would rush in from the garage, his shoulders sagging and his face grey with weariness, saying, 'I'm sorry. I'm sorry. I forgot. I was busy.' Too tired to argue she would pull herself up, and silently they would do the chores together and fall into bed.

Sometimes she thought back to her past life. It seemed like a dream: regular wage packets, plenty of food and the luxury of the search for meaning in life. Now there was no security, no fancy food and no wage packets. Now the only meaning was: how can we eat? How can we pay our bills? Every time she picked up her Bible to read it fell open at the same place. Day after day she read, 'Be strong and work: for I am with you, saith the Lord of Hosts.'[1] And so the work continued, endlessly grinding on. And on. And on. Women's Lib. never mentioned the agony of work, she thought.

One day she found Jonathan crying. 'My feet hurt. My

[1] Haggai 2:4

sandals pinch my toes!' he said. She put him on her knee. His first reaction after finding out that his father was out of work had been to pour out all his pocket money from the old jam jar on to her lap. Now she ruffled his hair. Later when he had gone to bed, she prayed quite simply, 'Lord, I know it's no use asking for new sandals for him, only Jonathan's feet hurt....'

A couple of days later a friend phoned up. 'Er...' would Jonathan like some new shoes? It's been on my mind and I'd like to buy him some.'

Jonathan was so excited when she told him that he said, 'I'd like to pray for a flowered shirt and matching tie as well!'

Jenny swallowed. 'I'm not sure....'

But he was already praying and confident.

A few days later her mother phoned up and said, 'A lady from church has given me some clothes for you.'

'Oh yes?'

'There's a beautiful flowered shirt and matching tie. Do you think Jonathan would like them? They're just his size!'

Jenny giggled suddenly. All this suburban adventure was taxing and testing, but there were lighter moments.

There came the day when she ran out of bread. She stared at the empty bread bin and sighed. It was half-day closing. They would have to have potatoes for supper and no toast for breakfast. 'Lord?' she began and then shook her head. Only people in the Bible prayed for bread. Just before tea the doorbell rang. Her beautiful friend, Debbie Jackson, was standing on the doorstep. Jenny stared at her, puzzled. In Debbie's arms was an enormous crusty bread loaf. They looked at each other. Debbie held out the bread. 'I expect you've got a bin full of the stuff. Only we were doing baking at school today and I just felt I *had* to bring it over.'

'Well *thank you*!'

There were other times, too; people gave them meat and honey and baskets of vegetables. And slowly summer came and somehow the money was stretching out. At last she saved up enough for their caravan holiday. When, finally, they flung themselves down on the beach, it was raining. Slowly Jenny took off her shoes, found two plastic bags, put them on her feet and then put her feet back into her shoes.

'What are you doing that for?' squeaked Debbie. 'You look awful!'

Jenny grinned. 'My shoes leak. And I'm determined not to get my feet wet.'

Jonathan said in a superior voice, 'Well I'm going to pray for the sun to shine and then your feet won't get wet and you can take those plastic bags off. I wouldn't be seen dead walking down the beach with you like that!'

Jenny gazed up at the grey skies and pale disc of sun covered with ragged clouds. She sighed. 'All right, dear,' she said and pulled her anorak closer for warmth. He ran a little way up the beach, bent his head for a moment and then scampered off. She shut her eyes. Poor little soul! How were they going to explain to him when the rain didn't stop. Suddenly she blinked. She found herself screwing up her eyes as she scanned the beach for the children. The clouds seemed to have parted just above her head and the sun was pouring through. First she took off her anorak and then, slowly, the plastic bags.

It was the beginning of the first—and last—heatwave of the summer. And it lasted for the whole two weeks they were on the island.

When they got back Francis rented the top floor of an old cotton mill in Stockport. The wooden floor was stained black with oil from the looms and down the corridors were dishes of rat poison. When Jenny saw it she said, 'Why are all your desks covered with sheets of plastic?'

'Er...the roof leaks!'

'But!'

'The rent's low!'

They began to laugh helplessly, leaning against the filthy walls. George Croston, who had joined them in the business, came out to see why they were laughing. 'Come on, you two,' he said, 'What's the joke?'

'You are a sort of David in a Goliath market place,' said Jenny at last. The three of them set off down the corridor for the lift. Jenny stopped suddenly and listened. The whole place hummed with the sound of machinery and men's voices and the blare of transistor radios. 'How many people work here?' she asked.

Francis said, 'There are about forty little firms that work here.'

'Forty!'

'Yes. And they're all thriving. They do everything from curtain material to light engineering.'

She looked back in astonishment at the sooty walls, and the bleak rooms and the draughty corridors with the rat poison. Yet all round her was the sound of music and singing, and machines whirring.

'Well,' said Francis after a moment, 'they're all thriving on a shoe string.'

She stopped dead in the yard. 'Francis, I remember reading in *The Daily Telegraph* recently that an economist said England's prosperity depends on small businesses. He said that if every small business took on just *one* extra person, there'd be *no* unemployment. It sounds too fantastic, I know.' She looked back to the old factory and its forty firms. 'Can it be true? Can it? Because if it is, and if our business goes well, we could employ people and give them a chance of work and....'

George and Francis began to laugh. 'Hang on,' said Francis. 'We've hardly begun yet ourselves. We may fail.'

'Yes, yes, I know that, but,' her gaze went back to the factory, 'if we did succeed I can't think of any better way to help people. All the talk and all the words on a Sunday wouldn't mean half as much as a decent job!'

'Come on,' said Francis and dragged her to the car. 'You and your imagination!'

As they drove home Francis said soberly, 'Look, Jenny, if our firm does do well, it'll be because the Lord has had his hand upon it. The glory will be his but we will have to work and work.'

Yes, she thought, if it prospers it will be because the Lord has blessed us. And into her mind slid the memory of their 'pictures' of long ago of the black valley and the black trees and them as a family disappearing from view. But they had come out of it. They had struggled through. She clasped her hands round her knees. If only their own survival could help others too. In a happy dream she imagined a group of men with smiling faces leaving the dole queue and being given a job making furniture with their hands. Carpenters, like Jesus....

All too soon they were at home. The washing-up needed doing, the clothes ironing and the children settling. She sighed. It was all very well having dreams! But the reality included an awful lot of hard work!

CHAPTER TWENTY-TWO

THE TIME FOR JOY

I spoke to the Lord and asked him
to show me what I was.

There was no answer in words.
Only the strangest of ideas came to
mind: I was like a bulb in summer.

At first I didn't understand. A
bulb is invisible
in summer, hidden under-
ground. It may as well be dead.
Or non-existent. It seems like a
nothing. I was bitterly
disappointed and turned to go.

'Don't forget next spring,' said
my Lord.

Diary
Jenny Cooke

One evening Jenny sat fidgeting over her evening meal, twisting her engagement ring round and round her finger.

'What's the matter?' asked Francis at last.

'I, well, they haven't paid me at the night school yet. The headmaster hasn't collected my pay signatures for weeks!'

He started to get up. 'I'll phone him for you,' he said wearily.

'No!'

'No?'

'No. I'll do it myself.' She set off for the phone. 'And,' she said over her shoulder, 'I suppose I'd better learn to drive as well.'

Eventually after phoning three times during that week she got her money... and an appointment with a driving school.

'What's brought all this on?' asked Francis mildly.

She frowned. 'I don't know. I just feel, right inside, that if I'm grown-up, I should be able to do things on my own.'

He laughed.

She said, 'It's easy for men to laugh. They do it without thinking. But it's amazing how many women I know who still daren't do...oh, lots of things. They lose all their confidence by being stuck at home with the children.'

He stopped laughing.

She said slowly, 'It's got nothing to do with a husband being head of a family. That's something else. But what I'm talking about is women in general and wives in particular being able to live the lives God wants them to live. Not being bound by old fears. There should be growth in a person's life. Development and....'

He settled down in his seat and his face wore a patient and 'I've heard it all before' look.

She said, 'You achieved all that before I met you. But I didn't. I was too young.'

'You mean a marriage should develop as the partners do?'

'Enriched is the word,' she said.

'Mmm. How?'

'Only one way I know.'

'You mean praying together?' he asked.

'Yes. And talking. Talking with each other a lot. Sharing at depth. And the annoyances too!'

'You're good at sharing those!'

She grinned. 'Well it's better than bottling them up. Anyway, women are good at communicating. Men need to learn the art of sharing from us!'

That weekend she had a dream. In the dream she was lurking in the shadows watching a well-known Christian leader organizing a meeting. Several times he turned in her direction and beckoned her. Still unsure of herself she hung back. At last he called out, exasperated, 'Well, are you coming over, or aren't you?'

Hesitantly she took a step forward.

'Come on, do!'

She walked up to him, but he was already busy with someone else.

'There,' he called over his shoulder. 'Get on with it. It's on the floor.'

In the dream she looked at the floor. There was a many-squared diagram spread out at her feet. Each square was dry and sandy, as dull as dust.

'But...,' she said.

Impatiently he came to her again. 'Well get on with you and pick up your square! Go on! I'm telling you to!'

'But...what is it?'

'It's a diagram of the history of the church.'

Suddenly he was gone.

She bent down and picked up her tiny square. It lay on her palm, as dry as dust. Tears welled up in her throat. What on earth was she supposed to do with it? It was boring. It was terrible. It was hopeless. It was...she swallowed her tears and turned sadly away. As she walked off she rubbed the square with her thumb and its arid edges rasped with dryness. All at once she stopped. She turned back. She looked at her hand. The square had vanished. In its place a small plant was growing. It grew and grew until it flowed all over her hand. It dripped with roots; new green leaves forged upwards and seed-cases were forming. And right at its heart was a single, beautiful, velvet-purple flower. As she stared in wonder at her hand, a spurt of joy flickered at her core. The joy bloomed. It flooded through her veins.

When she woke up the memory of the dream was strong. And the joy was even stronger. For days the joy stayed with her.

'What does it mean?' she asked Francis.

'What do *you* think it means?'

'I, I'm not sure.' She was silent. 'It couldn't mean, could it, that I'm a bit more creative than I thought, could it?'

After some weeks she dreamed another dream. This time she was walking in a dark and dour back street, searching and searching for the church meeting she knew she was going to attend. At last she left the black streets. The sun came out. Suddenly, the dream went into colour. She half ran, with the old familiar joy beginning to surge, past red-brick houses, until she came to a great modern cathedral, which was all stained glass windows with the sun shining through the glass, making the pavements glow with colour. She stopped. But then knew she had to go on.

Finally she found the meeting hall. It was modern. She opened the door. Inside it was shaped like a tiny half-amphitheatre, with seats fanning down to the dais at the bottom. The carpets were green, the seats a golden-teak colour. She stood by the door and watched the happy crowd milling around the speakers. Somehow she knew this was a meeting about the writing of books. Joy, peace and happiness surged up through her. As she stepped forward into the room she knew with all her heart that she was right to be there.

Again she woke up with the joy so strong. Again she asked Francis what it all meant. 'Does it mean it's right for me to be involved with writing?'

'It sounds more than that to me!' said Francis. 'It sounds

as if it's a very good idea!'

As she stared at him, wanting to trust his advice, she found herself thinking that she must be a very creative person, and then she squashed the thought almost before it had time to surface. Yet the phrase 'very creative' stayed in her mind: but how could she be, when she was such a failure at being a mother, at speaking to people about her faith, when she always made safe conversation? Her mind ran on its usual, negative channels.

All at once she stopped. She got up and looked out of the window at the garden bursting with spring flowers. Supposing she looked at herself in a completely different way? Instead of focusing on the failures, why didn't she concentrate on the opposite: that Christ loved her. Even her. That Christ had a redemptive plan for her life, not just salvation in heaven, but here and now as well; that everything about her could be and was being changed, because Christ was in her, the hope of glory. Her relationship with Jonathan was being re-made. She had not been dominated by the fear of childbirth. Many men and women had been to meetings in their house and some had heard the gospel. She had kept her integrity about believing in the special work of the Holy Spirit and lost popularity because of it. She led good Adult Education classes, her students passed their exams, she got opportunities to speak of her faith to them and had now been offered a new job teaching 'Creative Writing'. Francis' business was thriving and they had begun to have a wage packet again. She bit her lip. It was such a shift in her usual pattern of thinking, that it was like the whole axis of a personality being changed.

'You are being changed...from one degree of glory to another!'[1] Suppose it were really true and that's what faith was all about: growing spiritual fruits and gifts and graces. Walking tall. Knowing herself forgiven, loved and re-made; even liking herself and being her own friend.

She sighed. There were still two questions unresolved in her life. Her shoulders drooped. She knew she had failed at the church. God didn't use her to bring renewal to the church. A ghost of a smile hovered over her face. She

[1] 2 Corinthians 3:18 (Revised Standard Version)

shrugged. She was beginning to think that perhaps she had been a bit arrogant in ever thinking he would.

The other question was about writing. She glanced at all her files. She flipped through the *Renewal* magazines with her yearly articles in. She remembered working with Trevor Hill of the BBC on a play for Macclesfield Parish church. It had gone well, a fragment even being televised. For seven years she had searched to find what it was she wanted to do. Now she knew. She wanted to be a writer. For a further five years she had written, with a very modest success. But now all the doors seemed to be closing, and the rejection slips from the BBC and the women's magazines were mounting. She sighed deeply. It was all very well dreaming joyous, creative dreams. But what happened when reality was the very opposite, and was negative and rejecting? She shrugged and sighed again. It didn't help, not at all.

About a year later she went to a Christian Writers' day in Manchester at Brunswick Parish church. Robert Beale welcomed everyone in the foyer and then they surged forward into the church. As she went through the doorway, Jenny stopped dead. She stared round her in wonder. There were the golden-coloured seats fanning down in a tiny amphitheatre arrangement towards the speakers' dais at the bottom. People were pushing past her, but still she stood. There was the green carpet. There were the speakers ready to talk about writing books. She took a deep breath and felt the old joy spreading. It was the same as in her dream, the very same. But what did it all mean?

CHAPTER TWENTY-THREE

THE WAY OF THE CROSS

Jesus said, 'Woe to you when all
men shall speak well of you!'

Luke 6:26

One morning as Jenny welcomed her friends and neighbours to a Bible Study coffee morning and glanced round the circle of happy faces, all at once the room seemed to go a shade darker. She forced herself to carry on. She told no one. But her mind was suddenly alive to a new thought. No, she corrected herself. It was an old thought. A thought she had imagined had long ago been dead and buried.

'How do you know,' sneered the thought, 'how do you know God *really* is there, really is alive. How do you know? How? How? How?'

After her friends had gone home and she was flying through her housework the thought pounded on. 'You can't prove God exists. You can't. There's only one alternative: there's nothing there at all. Nothing. You exist for nothing!'

The horror of nothingness began to haunt her again, as it had done in her student days. Day by day she lived reasonably enough, but each night before she fell asleep, the full force of a dead-end universe wrapped itself around her, blotting out the light. And she knew she was terrified of this new, old-old knowledge.

One day she went with a friend to see a performance of *The Seagull* at the Rex theatre in Wilmslow. As the play unfolded with the sad search for meaning, and the characters wandered hopelessly about, some bored and some in anguish, Jenny gripped the edge of her seat. She knew what Chekhov was writing about. She knew, only too well. At the interval she burst out with, 'Oh, what's the point of it all? I've done everything. I've got a career of sorts, had two children, a boy and a girl. What is there left for me to do? I'm only thirty. But there's nothing left. Nothing! I'll just have to live out my next forty years. And then die!' Her friend said, 'I never knew anyone else thought like that!'

Later, as Jenny tried to get to sleep, she understood the fear of darkness as she had never known it before. In her teens it had been a question of being an atheist or a Christian. Now it was much worse and much, much deeper. No matter what she did or thought or said, death was lurking, inevitably, in the wings: the last and final enemy. She lay rigid in the bed and tried to work it out. How could she believe there was Nothing behind the universe when she had known the joy of the Lord in her heart for so many years? It didn't make sense. At last, as she tossed and turned, she realized that it was her mind that was troubled. Not her spirit. But her mind would not rest. She clenched her hands. Somehow there had to be a way through. She would have to find her way through to understanding. She leaned back against the pillows, her heart a pool of sadness. For now she had finally understood. She was mortal.

It was one Sunday evening some weeks later that she and Francis began their usual Sunday evening prayer time. After he had prayed she sat in complete silence. Into her mind came crowding unwelcome thoughts and memories. She bit her lip hard and swallowed the lump in her throat. It stayed there. She remembered the different church people and Christian leaders she had known over the past ten years. Their words had often been kind and helpful. Sometimes they had not been. When she refused to abandon her quiet stance over believing in the Holy Spirit, stinging barbed words had been hurled in her direction.

'You are the most dangerous woman in the church!'

'You believe in a heresy!'

'We don't want that kind of thing here!'

'You are a heretic!'

'You'll endanger your children's salvation.'

'You're doing the devil's work.'

'You have a devil!'

She bent her head. She remembered her stumbling replies, her silences, her scalding tears hidden from public view. She stared at her knees. The only good thing about it had been the slow dawning of her determination. She knew there was freedom of speech in England. So she would believe what she would believe. And no amount of cold-shouldering and blank stares would stop her. She had not caused any trouble and no one was going to change her mind for her. No one. God never asked anyone to bend so far backwards to accommodate others' opinions that they became a yes-man. He always granted a person their integrity. She stared at her feet. She would not be a man-pleaser. Oh, no. She would be a God-pleaser.

But all of a sudden the secret burden she had carried for over ten years overwhelmed her. Her heart rose up in a sudden bitterness against her Lord. She cried out so loudly that Francis was startled.

'Lord,' she cried, 'I'm finished! I'm ended. You've ended me! I've tried for ten years to bring renewal to the church. I've failed.' There was a pause. All the sadness in her seemed to burst into her throat. She struggled on. 'You've broken my heart, you, God of love. You God, you!'

There was a resounding silence. She refused to open her eyes. Then she said, 'You say in the Bible that you are the light of the world, but you've led me into darkness.'

She paused, her hands clenched. 'You say you are a God of love: but you've put a knife through my heart.'

She opened her eyes and gazed at the carpet.

Francis never moved.

She said, 'If you want any more to do with me, Lord, then you'll have to approach me! I can't do any more.'

With that she sat quietly by the fire, spent, as if by a great storm.

Francis said, 'You ought not to pray like that. It's....'

She shook her head. 'I'm sorry. I couldn't help it.'

He sighed. 'Shall I make you a cup of tea?'

She nodded.

A couple of days later, as she was tidying up the dining-room, she came across a Bible under a cushion. She stared at it. It was strange not to be on speaking terms with God. Perhaps the Bible might, after all, have something to say. She opened it and thumbed through the pages, not knowing what she was looking for. All at once the word 'darkness' caught her eye. She began to read:

He hath led me and brought me into darkness,
but not into light.
He hath set me in dark places,
as they that be dead of old.
He hath bent his bow,
and set me as a mark for the arrow.
But though he cause grief,
yet will he have compassion...
For he doth not afflict willingly nor grieve
the children of men.[1]

She sat in a daze for several minutes while the words of Jeremiah scored her brain. It seemed too incredible that her outburst of two nights before had been felt and written about by that sad and courageous prophet. She sat back in the chair. She didn't understand it at all, but she felt comforted.

In Holy Week they went to Roy and Margaret Moore's house in Bramhall for a slide show and supper. Roy chatted about his recent visit to Israel and then said casually, 'This is a picture of the Via Dolorosa. Christ walked along this way to Calvary.'

A hush fell in the room. Jenny stared unseeingly at the screen. All at once some of her questionings were answered. The long line of 'Whys?' that had begun at the Deaf School, and continued with the birth of Jonathan, and even stretched back as far as her lonely childhood and hated playground times, that long line of 'Whys' were suddenly put into focus. She blinked very rapidly and carefully set her face into pleasant lines, but in her heart she at last understood. Or partly understood, anyway.

It was the Way of the Cross. Didn't Jesus say, 'If anyone wants to come with me, he must forget self, carry his cross, and follow me.'[2] So that was what had been happening in her life. Without her knowing it she was on the way of the cross, following her Lord. It was the narrow way, the only way, Christ's way. She shuddered suddenly and tried to concen-

[1]Lamentations 3:2,6,12,32,33
[2]Mark 8:34 (Good News Bible)

trate on the slides. But the thought had to be faced. The way of the cross had only one ending.

Later that month they went to a great rally in the Free Trade Hall. The Christians shouted, danced, laughed and sang. There were stories of healings, of miraculous help and provision from God. Jenny felt so sad. Everyone else seemed to live in the resurrection life. Only she was for ever left on the hard way. She sighed. The meeting was light, frothy, unreal.

Then David Watson got up to speak. The great hall went quiet. He waited. He stood, a slight figure leaning on the rostrum. Jenny fought back her tears. A great victory sermon was more than she could face. He picked up his Bible. He read:

> All I want is to know Christ
> and to experience the power of his resurrection;
> and the fellowship of his sufferings;
> and become like him in his death;
> in the hope that I myself will be raised from death to life.[1]

Jenny leaned forward. His beautifully articulate voice rolled round the hall. 'The fellowship of his sufferings,' he said. 'The fellowship of his sufferings.'

Silence fell in the audience, the singing of choruses and hand clapping forgotten. David paused and then said quietly. 'Oh, yes, we all want to know "the power of his resurrection" and be involved with exciting things and being busy for God.' He paused again. 'We all want to see the miracles and healings and Day of Pentecost experiences of the resurrection life.' He smiled gently. 'But how many of us want to experience "the fellowship of his sufferings"?' There was dead silence in the audience, the former jollity wiped away by the quiet voice.

He smiled. 'But, good people,' he cried, 'the two things go together. You can't have the one without the other! If you want to know the resurrection life, then be prepared to join the Lord in his sufferings as well. And if there are any of you here who are filled with pain, and tears, and criticism from

[1]Philippians 3:10 (Good News Bible)

others and who don't know what on earth God is doing to you, then,' his voice rose to a great cry, 'then be at peace! For the Lord is surely dealing with you and leading you on to become like his Son.'

The silence was total now. Heads were bowed. Some people sniffed into handkerchieves. Some fidgeted. Jenny sat stock still and for the first time in months, felt the dawning of hope.

David came to the end of his sermon. He looked all round the room. 'Christ will lead you to share in his sufferings. If you let him. And Christ will allow you to share in his resurrection life as well. If you let him. But the one goes with the other.'

After Easter Jenny and Francis went to a Fountain Trust Arts Weekend in London. During the final Communion service there was a time of open prayer. While everyone was quiet she gradually became aware that in her mind's eye she could see the shadow of an empty cross. She tried to dismiss it and concentrate on the service. The shadow came nearer. She resisted it. Then, suddenly, she gave in. The cross got bigger. She could see now that it was made of roughly polished wood. Then it was next to her, at an oblique angle. Helplessly she sat in an attitude of prayer as someone she couldn't see began to push the cross into her. Now it was in. Her hands, arms and heart were on the cross piece. Her feet, her heart and her head were on the upright. Nailed. She couldn't move. Her heart was crossed over twice. Tears, such as she had never known, poured from her eyes. They spouted down her cheeks making a pool on her lap. And she sat helpless, with Francis holding one hand and Sylvia Lawton holding the other, while she saw in a great rush all her hopes and dreams of renewal and resurrection, of being 'used' in the church, of doing something for God, of being a writer, or of being anything at all, all suddenly nailed to the cross with her. Dead. Finished. Gone.

She bowed her head. The vision faded. The people on each side offered handkerchieves. She knew she would never be the same again.

PART FOUR

THE LORD OF THE HILL

When morning was up, they had him [Christian] to the top of the house and bid him look south; so he did; and behold, at a great distance, he saw a most pleasant mountainous country, beautified with woods, vineyards, fruits of all sorts, flowers also, with springs and fountains, very delectable to behold. Then he asked the name of the country; they said it was Emmanuel's Land; [it belonged to the Lord of the Hill] and it is as common, said they, as this hill is, to and for all the pilgrims. And when thou comest there, from thence, said they, thou mayest see the gate of the Celestial City, as the shepherds that live there will make appear.

The Pilgrim's Progress
John Bunyan

CHAPTER TWENTY-FOUR

'GIVE ME THIS MOUNTAIN!'

Caleb cried, 'I have wholly
followed the Lord my God...
I have waited forty-five years...
Now, therefore, give me this
mountain of which the Lord
spoke...'

from Joshua 14:6–15 (paraphrase)

JENNY LEANED BACK in the grass and let the July sun bake into her limbs. She closed her eyes. All the tiredness of the past three weeks soaked away in the warmth. Jonathan sprawled motionless beside her, drowsy in the heat. After a while she rolled over and opened one eye. He was gazing across the tiny lake, watching dragonflies skim the water.

'Jon?'

'Mmm?'

'It's lovely here, isn't it?'

He smiled. Then, 'Shall we see if the baby's all right, Mum?'

They sat up together and listened intently. There was no sound from the carry-cot.

'Well your Dad's supposed to be looking after her and Debbie, so don't worry, love.'

He stretched back, his legs long and sunburnt. She watched him without his knowing it. Soon he'd be a big boy. Then a teenager. After that, a man, living his own life. She shut her eyes a minute and tried to imagine it.

A thin wail split the air. She struggled to get up but he was already bounding away, eager to get the new baby up before Debbie got there first. Jenny grinned. The familiar sound of quarrelling was already erupting between them.

Later, in the car going home, she said to Francis, 'Peggy's coming round tonight.'

'I thought she had gone back to America?'

'No. Steve's gone back. But she and the children are still at Didsbury. She wants to come and see the baby.'

Jenny leaned her head on the car seat, thinking about

Peggy. Jenny had been baby-sitting for friends, and when they came home, they said, 'When we went to Peggy Noll's this evening and told her you were baby-sitting for us, she had just read one of your articles in *Renewal* and wants to meet you!'

Jenny had blushed.

'She wants to read all your work.'

When she and Peggy finally met they discovered they both had a love of words and books, all tumbled in together with a love of family and friends, and a love of God. So they began to meet regularly. Jenny sighed. It was such a pity they were going to have to be separated by the Atlantic. Tonight was their last but one meeting before Peggy went back to America.

When Peggy arrived she and Jenny sat in the living-room, taking turns to cuddle the baby.

'So you're going to call her Laura?' said Peggy.

'Yes. And you are going to be her godmother!'

Peggy smiled in delight and her soft American accent filled the room. 'It's a real shame I've got to go home to Pittsburgh and miss the christening.' Then she leaned forward. 'There's something I want to ask you Jenny. And Francis too.' Her voice was urgent.

Jenny looked at her.

'Well, Steve and I wondered if you and Francis and the children would like to come and visit us in the States. Have a holiday with us. And....'

Jenny went bright pink. She opened her mouth and closed it again.

'And you could lead a week-end at Steve's college. You know, do some talks on the Bible for the student wives. And do a literary luncheon!'

'What!' said Jenny faintly. 'But....' Her voice suddenly cracked and her eyes went very bright. 'You mean actually come to America?'

'Yes.'

'But... I've never been further than Anglesey for ten years! I've got so parochial in my outlook.'

They both began to laugh.

'How wonderful,' said Jenny at last. 'How absolutely wonderful!' She looked at Peggy. 'How did you know? It's been my secret dream to come to America for twelve years! I had the chance once...and turned it down.'

Peggy stared back at her. 'I didn't know,' she said. 'I didn't know at all. All I knew was that we really wanted to invite you and made up our minds to do so.'

They looked at each other and then Peggy said slowly, 'There's only one problem.'

'What's that?'

'The cost.'

'Oh.' Jenny frowned. She hadn't thought of that. She knew they hadn't any spare money for tickets.

Peggy said at last, 'I don't want to sound trite. Only if the Lord wants you to come, he'll provide the money for the fare. And we, and other friends, will provide you with hospitality.'

'Oh, Peggy, how can I thank you.'

'Don't worry about that. We want you to come!'

They were silent together in the rich way companions can sometimes be. Gradually the room grew darker and the baby slept. Peggy put her hand on Jenny's arm. She nodded towards the baby. 'Did you have a bad time?'

They looked at each other with complete understanding.

Jenny nodded. 'Yes,' she said quietly. 'But,' and her eyes gleamed, 'I've learned a thing or two in my old age! I made such a fuss in that labour room. I groaned and moaned and cried and carried on so as they were all dancing round me. And it took so long there were three changes of staff too!' She smiled tiredly. 'It's funny. I hid all my feelings when I had Jonathan and I suffered in my mind afterwards. And it took me five years to build up a good relationship with him. But when Laura was born, I had the confidence to show all my feelings.'

Peggy nodded. 'I know. I know.'

'And I hardly think of her birth now. Except for the end. That was good. She was born so quickly at the end and I nursed her straight away and they didn't take her away from me. And I had such joy in her. It made me want to burst into song! We watched the dawn come up together, both completely alone in the delivery room. I've felt joyful ever since.'

Peggy gazed at the sleeping child. '"Just an ordinary miracle",' she said softly.

'What!'

Peggy smiled slowly. 'It's Laurie Lee. He said that when he had a daughter born to him late in life.'

It was not until after half past two the following morning, when the baby settled after her night feed, that the realization began to dawn on Jenny. Tired as she was, she couldn't sleep, but sat bolt upright in the bed. It was Peggy's invitation that sparked off her mind.

She remembered that afternoon long ago at Weetwood Hall. She had known then that the Lord was calling her to let go of writing, to let go of teaching English, to let go of going to America, and, worst of all, let go of the man she had decided to marry. She was so angry, so determined to go her own way. She remembered her disappointment at giving up the teaching of English, of putting away her writing in a drawer, of saying good-bye to the American trip. She remembered the six months' battle to give up Tim.

Now she sat in the bed and her heart began to beat rapidly. She had been given back the dearest and best gift of all in Francis. But there was more. She taught English and Creative Writing at the Adult Education Centre and loved it. Now Peggy had asked them to go to America...which meant that three of the things she had given up had been given back to her! Suddenly she yawned. Sleep began to overtake her. She leaned back on the pillows. Would the Lord give her back the writing of books too? Or was that too much to expect? And what about the money for going to America? And so, thinking, she fell asleep.

Next morning, when everyone had gone to work and school and Laura was quiet, Jenny found herself pacing up and down the living-room. She tried to settle down and get lunch ready, but she only managed to get the table half set before she darted back into the living-room again. Her heart was beating fast. Dare she? Dare she? Or was she being daft? She tried sitting down, but shot up again. Words were pouring through her mind, pushing at her lips.

At last she stood still in the middle of the room. She began to speak. She found her hands were quivering and her legs trembling.

'Lord,' she said, 'I...I...thank you for giving me back

those three things. So wonderful. So unexpected. And....' The words were clamouring in her brain, but she stopped herself. Then she took a deep breath. 'Lord, there is something I'd like you to do for me. Something so big, I hardly like to ask. So big, it's like a mountain. Only, please, please, give it to me!' All the pent up longing of the years suddenly poured into her voice. She stretched out her hands. 'Please, please give me the writing of books. Let me do it! And let me be on the radio, with my words. I want...I want to write books with you in them, Lord. And I want my words to be heard and to be read. By ordinary people and sad people and lonely people and searching people.'

There was silence.

She waited and then bowed her head. Her voice was very quiet. 'And if you don't give it to me, I want you to know this. I won't mind. I won't be angry. I might be disappointed, but I'll still love you. Only...if I could choose, that's what I would choose!' Her voice rose again, strong and joyous. 'Only give it to me, Lord! Give me this mountain! And for the people of England, let there be books on every bookstall in the country, with Jesus stalking through the words. Challenging the readers, reaching them...!' She stopped suddenly. Now whatever had made her pray *that*? She stared for a long time at her hands. Then she whispered, 'Give me this mountain.'

CHAPTER TWENTY-FIVE

NOTHING ELSE COUNTS!

I love God and he loves me.
Nothing else counts.

Diary
Jenny Cooke

NOTHING HAPPENED. SOON Laura was one and then nearly two years old. Still Jenny wrote no books. Still she searched in vain on the ordinary bookstalls of English towns for Christian books.

One day a friend suggested she wrote to Edward England and send him a manuscript.

Jenny was interested. 'Who's he?'

'Oh . . . a very well known man in Christian publishing. He is, or was, a director of Hodder and Stoughton. He'll give you a chance!'

Jenny sucked her pen. Should she? Hesitantly she got out the note-paper and began a letter. Then the phone rang and she forgot her letter, until a few weeks later when she picked up the latest edition of *Renewal* magazine. She flipped through the pages and suddenly a paragraph caught her eye. It was short and to the point. When she had finished reading it her face was set. She showed it to Francis that lunch-time: 'Edward England regretfully asks people not to send him any more unsolicited manuscripts until further notice.'

'Oh,' said Francis.

'That's it,' she said. 'I'd better not send him anything after all. He must have got inundated.' She sighed. Her dream of becoming a writer was so old now and so long unfulfilled, that it was almost gone. Her drawer was full of rejection slips. Her heart was heavy with the dashing of hopes. Then she raised her head. There were plenty of other things to do around the house. She picked up a school photo of the children. Weren't they more important? She nodded fiercely to herself, grabbed a sweeping brush and swept the floor till it shone.

One Sunday at church, as she skimmed through the bulletin

sheet, a sentence caught her eye. She reread it slowly and shook her head. It couldn't be true! It must be a misprint: 'Eight hundred men attend Strangeways Chapel every Sunday morning, going to the several different services held there.' She read on: 'The Rev. Noel Proctor, Chaplain of Strangeways Prison, is coming to speak in Emmanuel Church, Didsbury, next Tuesday evening.' She stared at the page. It might be interesting to go and hear him.

But when the Tuesday evening came she was tired, the children weren't in bed and the house was untidy. She looked at her watch. It was half past seven. 'Francis,' she called, 'will you go to the meeting for me? And take notes, in case I can write the story up for *Renewal*.'

He didn't answer straight away. Then he said, 'No. You go. I'll do the children.'

'But....'

'You know you ought to go and hear him, don't you?'

'But....'

'Here are your car keys!'

She stared, opened her mouth to argue, closed it again, caught his eye, suddenly relaxed and said, 'Oh, all right then. Thanks.'

She scrambled into the meeting just before it began. She stared at Noel Proctor and wondered about the eight hundred prisoners. But as soon as he opened his mouth and his soft Irish accent filled the air, she knew why the eight hundred men came to hear him.

After five minutes she was on the edge of her seat. The audience didn't know whether to laugh or cry. First he told one joke, then another. After that there was a pause and he told the story of the tragedies in his life.

'First my Dad died as a result of an IRA bomb blast in the Falls Road. He had been ill in bed and the shock killed him. And I thought to myself, why couldn't they leave an old man alone? He's never harmed anyone. And at that time I was a Chaplain at Eastchurch Open Prison and God knocked away all the props in my life: the prop of my parents, for my mum just gave up wanting to live after my dad died. Then the prop of religion went, the prop of the church and even the prop of the Bible. None of it seemed to mean anything to me any more. But worst of all, tragedy hit my family too. Because first my wife—Norma—her mother had a stroke, then Norma had a miscarriage, then my mother-in-law had another stroke and came to live with us. But Norma,' he stopped for a minute. Jenny gazed at him.

'Norma took cancer of the breast and she knew she was dying. And after that her mother died.'

The room was completely silent. Noel said, 'I thought I was losing Norma as well and I couldn't understand what the Lord was doing in my life. After all the work I had done for God. All the props were swept away.'

He looked at them all in their neat circle. He dropped his eyes and said, 'Something in me died.'

As Jenny listened she knew she understood. She knew what it meant to have God break one's heart and everything fall crashing round one's ears until there was nothing left. Nothing but you and God. And precious little of you left either.

She listened, sitting on the edge of her seat, as he swept the audience on: his time at Dartmoor, working with long-term prisoners; the revival during the Easter Mission there; the huge numbers being influenced at Strangeways. And Norma, clinging with faith to the Lord's promise to her that she was not to die, going up to Christie's hospital every six months for her check-up.

Jenny sat on afterwards, while conversations eddied around her. What a story! 'It would make a wonderful book, Lord,' she thought. She sighed, got up and went over to meet Noel. 'I'd like to write about you,' she said. 'An article for *Renewal*.'

He stared back at her and his eyes danced with merriment. 'So that's why you've been doing all those sheaves of notes! I thought you were checking up on my behaviour!'

She giggled suddenly and he laughed back at her. Then they were quiet.

'Well, see what comes of it,' he said at last.

Next morning there were more rejection slips through the post for her. During the week she got replies from different editors politely refusing her. She got out the Noel Proctor notes and flipped through them, then she pushed them away, too disheartened even to try again with his story. Apart from *Renewal* every door was closing. At last she said to Francis,

'Look, I've made my mind up. I'm finished with writing. I must have made a mistake. Obviously the Lord hasn't been leading me at all.'

He said, 'Don't be too hasty.'

'Hasty! I've been trying to become a writer for seven years. And for seven years before that I was so miserable because I didn't know what it was I wanted to do. Now,' she shrugged and slowly crumpled up the pile of rejection slips in her hand, 'now I know what I want to do. But it's not worked out. All the religious publishers and magazines have their own writers. The big secular publishing houses only accept one or two unsolicited manuscripts out of about seven hundred they receive every year. And the media have the whole world knocking at their door.' She threw the papers in the bin. 'So what chance do I have? I may as well face facts and forget the whole thing!' She took the bin out to the dustbin. He didn't try to stop her.

When she came back she said, 'You bought me that lovely Edwardian desk. I'm really sorry I won't be able to use it now. I feel I've let you down.'

He said, 'I bought it for you in faith. You'll use it. You'll see.'

She looked at him. She saw his face lined with weariness from a bad day at the factory. She saw his hands, calloused from working with wood and glue and saws. She saw his briefcase bulging with plans for special designs. She saw him reach for the teatowel to help her. And quite suddenly she understood. She loved Francis and he loved her. She loved her family and friends and they loved her. She stood very still for a moment. She loved God and he loved her. Nothing else counted beside all that. Her shoulders relaxed. She grinned.

'Oh, what does it matter about writing some daft old book, anyway!' she said.

And so, at peace together, they tackled the mammoth washing-up.

She woke up late next morning. Her head ached and her voice rose to match.

'Mum's at it again,' muttered Jonathan, deftly avoiding a smack, as he raced round the kitchen with one shoe on.

She grabbed the boiling kettle and began to make a pot of

coffee. 'Will you kids hurry up!' she shouted. 'You'll be late for school! Why don't you get up in a morning when you're called!'

Francis walked in and thrust a letter at her. 'Who do you know in Tunbridge Wells?'

'Don't be silly,' she said irritably and then looked at the postmark. 'No one. I don't know anyone who lives there.'

She pushed it away. 'I can't be bothered with letters now...oh, very well. I'll open it!'

She sat down with a thump and slit open the letter.

All at once her whole world went still. She stared at the single paragraph in the letter. The children went very quiet. It seemed as if time stopped. She got up and then sat down again.

'Francis,' she said, 'It's....'

'What is it, Mum?' said the children.

'It's a letter from....'

Francis came over and said, 'Who?'

She looked at him. Her bad temper, tiredness and headache were all forgotten. A great smile broke out all over her face. 'It's from Edward England.'

Francis opened his mouth, laughed and said, 'Well go on then! Read it to us!'

She glanced at the letter again and with a tremor in her voice read, 'He says, "Dear Jenny Cooke, I've read your articles in *Renewal*.... Would you like to write a book?... If so, I can arrange it for you.... Yours sincerely, Edward England." '

'Just like that!' said Francis. He grabbed the letter and read for himself. The kitchen erupted with noise and laughter and excitement.

Long after they had all gone to work and school she sat with the letter in her hand. Would she like to write a book? Would she indeed!

CHAPTER TWENTY-SIX

'ORDINARY' IS THE WRONG WORD!

Enough! The
Resurrection,
A heart's-clarion! Away grief's
gasping, joyless days, dejection.
Across my foundering
deck shone
A beacon, an eternal beam...
In a flash, at a trumpet
crash,
I am all at once what Christ is,
since he was what I am, and
This Jack, joke, poor potsherd,
patch, matchwood, immortal
diamond.
Is immortal diamond.

That Nature is a Heraclitean Fire
and of the Comfort of the Resurrection
Gerard Manley Hopkins

HER EXCITEMENT LASTED all that day. In the evening she spoke to Edward England on the phone.

'What do you want to write about?' he said.

'Er....'

'Have you met any interesting people lately?'

'Er...no. Oh, yes I have! I've heard Noel Proctor at church.'

There was a curious silence on the phone. She waited, wondering.

Edward said, 'When I was up in Manchester last year I went to the Christian World bookshop. The owner, John MacDonald, told me about Noel Proctor. I only had an hour to spare and decided it was hopeless to try and meet him. But a few minutes later he walked right into the shop!'

'Oh,' said Jenny, her heart beginning to beat faster.

'I asked Noel if he'd be willing for a book to be written about him and he agreed in principle. Only we couldn't find an author to do it. We couldn't find an author who lived near enough. We've been waiting for a whole year to find the right author!'

There was another silence on the phone. Jenny stood stock still.

Edward said, 'Would you like to write Noel's story, Jenny? It'll be a lot of work, but a wonderful opportunity.'

'Oh yes,' she said. 'I would. Oh thank you. Thank you very much.'

Her excitement lasted all night and most of the next day. But by late afternoon she'd begun to bite her lip. By the time Francis came home she had made up her mind. He took one look at her face and strode over. 'What's the matter now?' he said.

She reached for the kettle switch and turned it off blindly. Then, quite suddenly, she broke down. Her tears streamed all over the cup of tea she was making for him. 'It's no good,' she said at last. 'I'll have to turn the Noel Proctor book down!'

'What!' He grabbed the tea in one hand and her in the other. He searched her face with his eyes. 'Why?'

She gestured to Laura toddling round the kitchen, her plump face smeared with chocolate, and a scattering of toys behind her. 'Because,' said Jenny, 'I just *can't* put her in a nursery. She's not even two years old yet.'

'What's nursery got to do with it!'

'Because,' and Jenny twisted her hands, 'I've realized today how much work and time it'll take to do the book as it should be done. It'll take hours and hours and hours.' She shook her head. 'I just can't do it *and* look after Laura. And I can't bear to send her to a nursery. She's so sweet and I longed to have a third child. Now I've got one, I can't just push her to one side, so as I can fulfil my dream.'

She blew her nose and looked at him hopelessly. 'I'll ring up Edward this evening and tell him.' She started to get up to find the Tunbridge Wells phone number.

'Sit down!' said Francis. His voice was quiet but there was a hint of steel in it as well. She stopped, sat down again and waited.

'I won't allow it!' he said, drawing himself up to his full six feet. 'I won't allow you to turn it down!'

'What!' she said faintly.

'You don't pray for something for fifteen years, just to turn it down!'

'But...how will we manage? What about Laura?'

He frowned. 'I don't know. And she's *not* going to a nursery. I don't know how we'll manage or what we'll do. But,' and his voice was firm, 'you are doing that book! I don't want to hear any more nonsense about turning it down! Understood!'

'But...' she said, with a brighter look in her eye, 'But....'

'No "Buts"! You helped me to get the business going. Now I'll help you!'

'But we'll be exhausted and....'

He said, 'We'll do it by faith. Do you understand? You'll write the book by faith.'

There was silence between them.

Then he said, 'What will you need so you can do it?'

She thought fast. 'The ideal thing would be a paid helper in the house. A nice girl, perhaps unemployed, to care for Laura in the afternoons.'

'Right. We'll pray about that then. And we'll ring up a few friends and ask.'

'But....'

'No more "Buts"! Now what's for tea?' And he strode from the room, whistling as he went. She stared after him, her tears all dried up. And with the beginnings of a smile, she set to work on the vegetables.

By the following lunch-time she was hopping up and down in excitement. She rang Francis up at work. 'You'll never guess what!'

'What?'

'The very first person I rang up was Jane Powell. You know, my Gatley friend.'

'Yes. Go on.'

'Her daughter would like the job! Afternoons looking after Laura would suit her fine as she's got morning jobs elsewhere! She's been praying to find work before she takes up her nursing training next year!'

He chuckled. 'You see. I told you it would work out!'

'But so often things haven't worked out in the past.'

He groaned. 'Just be thankful this has!'

'Yes, dear.' She laughed. 'See you later!'

But even with Francis so solidly behind her, and her mother coming over one day a week to help, and Alison Powell proving to be such a wonderful person in their home and even with Laura being so contented and happy, Jenny found herself quite unprepared for the whirlwind of words that began to pour into the tape-recorder.

Every other Tuesday she and the Proctors got together, prayed, had a meal and then they talked. Noel and Norma talked, and remembered and chuckled over their past life and the tape-recorder faithfully took down every word.

It was only when Jenny got home and began to transcribe their words, phrase by phrase, that she realized the extent of the job she had been given. Noel's voice and very turn of speech began to replay itself in her mind. She fell asleep with their voices running through her thoughts. She woke up next morning and their words were ringing in her ears.

Slowly she built up a massive file of transcripts; of sermons; of old black and white photographs from their Belfast and Darlington days. She studied the photos. She absorbed them. She watched programmes about the Falls Road on television. She shut her eyes and imagined Noel walking down them or cycling to the Royal Victoria Hospital. And she prayed constantly.

She found that if she got up at seven in the morning and worked till eleven at night for six days a week and gave herself no breaks, no relaxation with books and no relaxation with television, and if she cut out all mid-week church meetings and all coffee mornings and everything she had ever, ever done—if she did all that in faith, then the book grew, her children were content, and she could sleep easy at nights. But the cost was high.

'All the new friends I've made at Didsbury,' she said to Francis. 'I have to keep turning down their invitations. Whatever will they think? I try and explain, but it sounds so feeble.'

He said, 'Just do the book, Jenny. You've promised Edward England, and the Proctors and the publishers. You've got no choice.' She gritted her teeth. The August deadline she had agreed to was getting nearer.

Day after day in those months she waited to hear Alison's key in the lock. Laura heard it too and trotted, chortling, up the hall. Then, when she knew they were both settled, she began the climb upstairs. Alison watched her one day as each foot trod heavily and slowly.

'How on earth do you do all that work, Jenny? Don't you get fed up?'

Jenny smiled tiredly. 'When I'm at the bottom of the stairs, the last thing I want to do is drag myself up, go into our bedroom and sit at my desk and pull out the old typewriter and know there's three or four hours work ahead of me.' She looked at her hands. There was a writers' callous on the middle finger of her right hand. 'Only somehow I just force myself to do it. And do you know! It's amazing! Because in no time at all it's half past five and my pen has skimmed over loads of pages and I feel so really happy. I can't explain it.' She laughed. 'This is what comes of me praying all those prayers! I'll know better next time.'

Alison laughed too. 'Me and my mum and dad think it'll be a bestseller,' she said shyly.

Jenny went pink. 'I don't know about that,' she mumbled and turned to climb the rest of the stairs.

It was when she was deep into the book and the February days were dark that the slow understanding came to her. She put down the pen and stared at the page. It was as if every difficult experience she had ever had was preparing her to write this book. Even teaching new subjects at night school had been preparation. It had taught her how to work quite independently and plan out whole courses of work with no previous knowledge of a subject. She chewed her pen. No. It was the other way round. It was because she understood about miscarriage and therefore losing a child; and about physical pain, agony even; and having no work; and then prayers not being answered; and then having too much work. It was because she knew about all that, that she could write about the Proctors and get under their skin. It was because she knew what it felt like to die inside that she could write about Noel's similar experience.

She drew a deep breath. All her questionings about being ordinary were suddenly answered. She had been called to be ordinary, so that she could understand other ordinary people. Only 'ordinary' was the wrong word. It was a call to be human and drink the cup of human experience. She grinned. Best not to wax too eloquent on the theme or else Francis would say she was 'at it again'!

But as she got up to go downstairs and stretch her tired limbs and cramped fingers, new thoughts hit her. It was because she had come to terms with her bitterly lonely childhood, and had had problems with her son, and a broken engagement and suffered with darkness in her mind, that she knew she understood the halting stories of the prisoners. And the stories that other people often shared with her as well. She simply understood. That was it. The Lord had allowed all that pain in her life...so that she could find the understanding. Then that meant nothing had ever happened to her by chance. Nothing.

She got up from the desk, covered the typewriter and put away her pens. Slowly she trudged downstairs, but her head was held high. For the first time in many years she caught the snatch of a glimpse of what it meant to be fully human. And fully Christian. And the cost of it, and the joy of it, staggered her.

CHAPTER TWENTY-SEVEN

THE KEY OF PROMISE

Giant Despair told Christian and Hopeful that since they were never likely to come out of Doubting Castle, their only way would be forthwith to make an end of themselves, either with a knife, halter or poison: 'For why,' said he, 'should you choose life, seeing it is attended with so much bitterness?'

Some days later Christian cried, 'What a fool am I thus to lie in a stinking dungeon when I may as well walk at liberty! I have a key in my bosom, called Promise, and that will, I am persuaded, open any lock in Doubting Castle.'

The Pilgrim's Progress
John Bunyan

JENNY CLIMBED INTO her car and took the road to Macclesfield. Her papers and files were stacked in the front. Laura was grizzling on the back seat. Finally she arrived at her parents' bungalow. Her mother let her in with a happy smile. 'We've got everything ready for you, dear,' and she led Jenny into the back bedroom. A chair and a baize-topped card table had been placed there. 'You can get on with your book and I'll take Laura to the park.' 'And I,' said the big voice of her father, 'will do your typing for you. Hurry up now and give it to me!'

She went into the lounge. His typewriter was ready.

'Thanks, Dad.'

She turned to her mother, 'Oh, Mum, I'm so grateful. To both of you. These last few weeks I've not known if I'm coming or going!'

Her mother smiled. 'Get yourself some coffee and then forget us. We won't disturb you. Lunch at one o'clock. Okay?'

'Lovely.'

Jenny went into the back bedroom. She opened her file and stared at the pages. The words danced up and down in front of her eyes. She set out her pages with care. But all of a sudden she buried her head in her hands. 'I can't go on,' she said silently. Her parents were being so good to her. And now she was going to let them down. 'I can't go on.'

She lifted her head up and groaned. It was there again. She put her hand up and tried to push it away. It stayed. She blinked her eyes very rapidly. It didn't move. What on earth was happening to her? Was she going mad? She gazed fixedly at the object that was just within the line of her vision. She passed her hand in front of her eyes. So it wasn't there really. It was only a figment of her imagination. But the more she tried to forget it, the more it taunted her.

She pushed her files away. She *had* to do something and quickly, before it was too late. She gave her attention to the object that haunted her mind's eye. It was a bottle of pills. 'Take me,' said the pills. 'Swallow me. Then you'll be free of all this work. You can rest. You can die.' The pills seemed to mock her. 'Who do you think you are? Who'll read this book? It's a silly book. You're foolish. Big-headed. It'll be a terrible failure. Everyone will laugh at you. No one will like you.'

She gazed mesmerized, at the bottle with its insidious message. Yes. It would be so easy, so easy to.... She pulled herself together sharply. 'Stop it! Stop it!' she said to herself. 'I won't give in. I mustn't. I....' But the pills stayed there. They had been there every waking moment for fourteen days. Each morning she had got up and they were there. They stayed with her as she went to the shops, as she stood outside the hardware store and tried to concentrate on how many light bulbs she needed to buy. She tried to ignore the bottle and forget it. But it stayed. And now she didn't know what to do. Only she felt so tired, so weary of fighting, so ready just to rest and rest and forget everything. Once she had tried to ring up a lady at church, but after three rings she had put the phone down again. Who would believe her? They would think she was going off her head.

All at once she sprang up. The pills seemed to grow bigger and bigger. 'Take me,' they murmured. 'Take me, or your children....'

She spun round and faced the taunting voice. 'My children are protected by God,' she cried, 'and get away from me, you tempter, you!'

Something changed in the room. There was a shift in the darkness that surrounded the bottle of pills. Suddenly she picked up her manuscript and read out loud what she had written. It was the exposure of witchcraft and evil powers, about a cell being exorcized and prisoners being set free from bondage to evil spirits, and from a curse. Set free by the power of Jesus Christ.

She took a deep breath and still standing said aloud, 'I will not change a single word on my page. I will write what I will write. And *nothing* will make me change my mind. So in the name of Jesus Christ, get away from me you evil one. I claim the protection of the Lord's precious blood.'

'Who do you think you are?' sneered the retreating voice behind the pills. 'You nothing! You nobody!'

'That's as may be,' said Jenny, advancing slightly into the room, 'but you aren't fighting me. You fight three others who dwell in me: the Father, the Son, and the Holy Spirit. You can't beat them.'

All at once the room was empty of darkness. The sneers vanished. The pills were gone. She sat down and with a determined jut of the chin, picked up her pen again. After a moment she put it down. She bowed her head. Her lips moved for a while. Then, as peace and happiness once again established themselves in her heart, her pen began to race across the page.

A couple of weeks later Jenny arrived outside the Proctors' house and flew up the path. Her file was fat with the book now. There was only the ending left to do. She rang the bell and then hesitated. How was she going to end a book when the Proctors were still in the middle of living it all?

When at last Norma answered the door, her face didn't have its usual smile. 'Come in, Jenny,' she said, her shoulders hunched.

Jenny stared at Norma and then cleared her throat. But Norma spoke first. 'You've heard the News, I suppose.'

'The News?'

'Yes. It was on the News last night.'

'No. I don't know.'

Norma blew her nose. 'There's been a cell fire at the prison. Noel's really upset. I can't do anything with him. See if you can say something to him.'

Jenny said, 'Would you rather I came back later?'

'No! No! It'll take our mind off it if you're here. Go on in and I'll make the coffee.'

Jenny stood at the lounge door a moment and then looked back at Norma. Norma said, 'Three prisoners have died.

They couldn't get them out of the cell in time.'

Jenny bit her lip, knocked on the door and went in quickly. Noel was pacing up and down the room, up and down.

'Oh, Jenny, hello there. We're glad to see you this morning.'

He sat down suddenly and put his head in his hands. Then he blew his nose and looked at her. He said, 'I feel a complete failure. It's my fault. I've failed those men.'

'No,' said Jenny. 'No.'

'One of them was having counselling. He wanted to join a Bible Study group.' He looked at her and his eyes were red with weariness. 'He died at three o'clock on Sunday morning. I was with his mother at the hospital.' Noel shook his head. 'Everyone's so upset at the prison. And I don't believe those three young men meant to commit suicide. I think they did it as a protest. Conditions are so bad. And it got out of hand. Fire and fumes go up so quickly.' He got up and paced up and down again. 'It's no good you writing a book about me, Jenny, when I've failed those three men.'

'No,' said Jenny. 'You haven't.'

Norma came in. The three of them looked at each other. Jenny looked at the fat file and then at the tape-recorder. Norma opened her mouth, but Noel got in first. 'I suppose we'd better get down to work,' he said slowly. 'After all we can't let young Jenny down, can we?'

'No,' said Norma. 'We can't.'

'If you're sure you want to carry on today?' asked Jenny.

Noel said, 'We've got to keep going somehow.'

'Yes.'

They went quiet. Then the three of them bowed their heads over the fat file. They stayed like that for some time. Each of them prayed. Then Noel said, 'I think I'll give you the tape of Sunday morning's service, Jenny. When the Governor and I had to speak to the prisoners about the cell fires.' She nodded.

When she got home she listened to the tape. She played it again. And a third time. Afterwards she sat, as if turned to stone. She opened her file and looked at the ending she had planned for the book. It was to be a successful ending: Noel the popular Chaplain, a revival of interest in Christianity at the prison, Norma pronounced cured of cancer at Christie's hospital, Strangeways featured on BBC1's *Songs of Praise*.

That would be a fine ending and a true one. As a chapter it could still go in. But it wasn't the only truth about the prison. She stared again at the tape. Dare she? Dare she end with a tragedy, that threw into stark relief all Noel's work and effort, and all the agony and work and problems of the prison staff and the prisoners? Instead of being a safe ending, it would be open-ended—like life. She took down her Bible and reread the ending of the Gospels. Slowly she picked up her pen. She knew what she was going to do.

When finally the book was finished she asked Noel and Norma to vet the last chapter carefully.

'We'll ring you back,' they said, taking the enormous file with them. 'The Governor will have to see it as well.'

Noel phoned her a couple of days later. 'It's absolutely fine,' he said. 'We both think it's the right ending.'

'And the epilogue as well?'

'Yes. Jenny?'

'What's that?'

'The Governor's seen it. Actually, I thought he'd keep it a week.'

'What did he say?' she asked, her heart in her mouth.

Noel paused. 'He said he normally *never* reads a religious book. But he had a lot of reports to do, so he thought our book would be a bit better than them!'

'Oh?'

'But he said he couldn't put it down. He said he was up till two o'clock this morning with it! He likes the ending too and the title. And....'

'Yes,' she said, a lump so big in her throat that it hurt to swallow.

'He says he thinks it's a fine book and he's very pleased, and he thinks a lot of the lads in prison will read it and that it will mean something to them and that he thinks we've been very honest and....' He ran out of breath. 'And he wants to know how this Jenny Cooke got the atmosphere so right when she's never been inside. And he wants you to know he's quite impressed!'

She couldn't speak for a moment. All her hours and hours

of work were suddenly, gloriously worth while. An important man like the Governor had said all that, when everyone knew he called a spade very much a spade!

'Oh, Noel,' she said at last, 'We'll probably never get any better praise than that!'

It was some weeks later that she got a cheque from the publishers. When she was speaking to Edward on the phone she mentioned it. 'I didn't expect it,' she said.

He laughed. 'It's only what you deserve. If you'd worked all those hours in secular employment you'd have got far more.'

After she put the phone down, she stared at the cheque. Even if she gave a proportion away, there would still be enough....

'Francis,' she cried and rushed downstairs.

He looked up, startled. Her face was bright with excitement. 'We can go to America after all!' She waved the cheque at him. 'We can go to the New World. After all these years I can go to America!' She danced a jig on the rug. 'We can see Peggy and Steve, and fly in a Jumbo jet and visit Washington and see Niagara Falls and...!'

He said, 'What a great idea!'

And afterwards, as they went to buy the tickets, the trip to America seemed like a glorious reward, after all their years of failure, struggle and work.

CHAPTER TWENTY-EIGHT

A TIME TO REAP

Let those who wept as they sowed
their seed
Gather the harvest with joy!
Those who wept as they went out
carrying the seed
Will come back singing for joy
as they bring in the harvest.

Psalm 126:5–6
(Good News Bible)

THE PHONE RANG and Jenny answered it. 'Yes?'

'It's me! Francis.'

'Hello!'

'I couldn't wait to tell you!'

'What! What is it?'

His voice came strongly over the phone. 'I expect he was flannelling me really!'

'Do *tell* me!'

'Well, you know my Bank Manager's leaving. He took me out to lunch today.'

She closed her eyes. In her mind's eye she saw the massive marble portals and heard the hushed atmosphere of the Manchester bank. 'How did you get on in the corridors of power, then?' she asked.

Francis cleared his throat. 'Well no doubt he was in a good mood, but...do you know what he said to me?'

'No! The suspense is killing me!'

'He said that our firm had been one of the top ten in Manchester he had to deal with!'

'What!'

'Not in size, of course. But in his estimation. He said he wished they were all like ours.'

She said. 'Oh, Francis! How lovely for you. How very, very nice of him.'

'I told you it was all flannel!'

She laughed. 'Maybe. And maybe not. But I'm very pleased all the same.'

After she had put the phone down she stared thoughtfully at the receiver. She and Francis were under no illusions about the firm. It could only last as long as the orders lasted. If the orders dried up, they would be finished. And their home would be gone into the bargain. Only, as Francis so often said, the Lord helped him. The orders didn't dry up, but ever so steadily increased.

She remembered the beginnings of the business in their grimy garage. Then there were all the problems they had had since: Francis being taken to Court by a former employee for unfair dismissal. Francis going to the Appeal Court in London and she trying to stop him.

'You'll never win!' she'd said.

And he'd frowned and said, 'I don't care! It's my right as an Englishman. I'm free before the Law. And I'm innocent, so I'm going to defend myself!' And his smile when he came home that night. 'I won,' he'd said and then sighed. 'But I still feel sorry for the other chap.'

There had been other problems too. Big companies going bankrupt, owing huge debts; firms trying to copy their designs without permission. But always there was the steady stream of orders and Francis saying, 'As long as the Lord wants this firm to exist, he'll bless it with orders.' Then there was all the work and Francis getting up at five o'clock in the morning with new designs bursting in his head.

She remembered the good things too: the wonderful dozen or so people who worked for them faithfully; some had been unemployed before coming to their firm and were so thankful for a job. And then the happy day when Francis and his designs had been accepted as worthy of belonging to the Guild of Master Craftsmen.

The firm was a vision they had had long ago. And the Lord had blessed them. There had been an agony of work and the toll on them was great. But Francis was seeing it through. It was good and she clasped her hands. It had given people work and purpose and some of them had become Christians as well.

A week later she and Francis and the Proctors were sitting in the faded elegance of the Midland Hotel. A massive pile of their book, *The Cross Behind Bars*, was in one corner. Television cameras and harassed reporters clustered round them. The new Governor of Strangeways prison told a funny story about Dartmoor. The Deputy Chief of Police chatted to Francis over a cup of coffee. Later Jenny watched as Noel was interviewed first for Granada and then for the BBC.

A *Manchester Evening News* reporter came up to interview her. After a moment he sucked his pencil. 'I've never heard of anything like this before,' he said, gesturing towards the pile of books. 'But I think it's great what you're trying to do.'

After that a *Daily Telegraph* reporter came up and said, 'What a super book!' His eyes twinkled. 'I was up late last night, trying to finish it!' He nodded. 'There'll be a report about it in my paper!' The noise and hustle and bustle of the Press Conference seemed to go on all the morning, until at last they escaped into the sunshine of the Manchester streets.

After lunch, on her own in the kitchen, Jenny switched on the radio. The beautiful voice of Lesley Judd floated into the room and a minute later she was interviewing Noel. Jenny listened and suddenly her knuckles went white as she heard her book, title, author and all being read out on the mighty *Woman's Hour*.

On the Saturday she and Francis drove into Manchester again for a signing session at the Scripture Union bookshop. On the way she said, 'Francis, dare we, I mean, would it be silly to go and look at the big secular bookshops?'

'Why not!'

So they strolled into Sherrat and Hughes, feet going carefully, slowly, but eyes darting here, there and everywhere. The first thing that caught her attention was an enormous display of Cliff Richard's new book, bang in the middle of the shop. *You, Me and Jesus*, she read. She pulled Francis on the arm. 'Francis, how terrific! Cliff's book will be in every bookshop in England!'

And her heart gave a leap as she suddenly remembered her prayers for the bookstalls and bookshops of England. After a while they found a neat pile of her own book at the back of the shop on a middle shelf. She grinned. The cover certainly looked good. There were other Christian books there too.

Francis looked at his watch. 'Just time to go to W. H. Smiths in the Arndale Centre.'

They went into the shop and stared about them. Hundreds and hundreds of titles stared back. They walked over to the religious bookshelf. Her book wasn't there. They went upstairs. They looked. At last she said in a small voice, 'Come on. It's not here. I must have been mad thinking it would be and....'

All at once she stopped dead. The noise and bustle in the shop faded away. She clutched him by the arm and pointed. Her hand trembled a little. She found she couldn't speak. He followed her gaze and then, in complete silence they walked towards the display shelf next to the till. 'Top Ten Paperbacks!' blared the display shelf. 'Top Ten Paperbacks!' And there, in the midst of the famous and infamous paperbacks beloved by England's readers, shone the title and cover of *The Cross Behind Bars*.

Suddenly they both began to laugh, and laughing helplessly like two teenagers, they turned and bolted out of the shop. When at last they found Noel signing a pile of books at the Scripture Union shop, he said, 'Apparently the first edition is almost sold out already. They are planning to reprint already!'

'What!'

'Yes! Ten thousand books have nearly gone!'

'But it only came out yesterday!'

The three of them began to laugh. Then Noel nodded. 'It's true,' he said.

'I just can't believe it,' said Jenny.

'Neither can I!'

On the way home she said to Francis, 'It's an awfully good thing there's a pile of ironing for me to do at home. And potatoes to peel, and washing and mending. Otherwise I might start swanning around and getting too big for my boots!'

'I shouldn't worry about that!' he said.

'Why not?'

'Because if you do there's four of us at home ready to squash you!'

'Well thanks a lot!' she said.

And so, laughing and excited, they bowled home.

When they arrived she ran upstairs into their bedroom and shut the door. She stood in silence for a few moments and then reached for her Bible. She opened it, looked down and read. Words seemed to jump from the page. 'Fear not.... Be glad and rejoice,' she read. 'For the Lord will do great things.'[1] She stared at the words for some time. She felt so happy, as if she were a child again, being given the best Christmas present in the world. She dashed away tears of joy from her cheeks. It was as Francis had said. The Lord had blessed her and the Proctors. Without the Lord none of it could have happened. The Lord had his hand upon the book and the glory was his.

There was a sound of chuckling on the stairs. She ran and opened the door and saw the family crowded round. Debbie ran up and kissed her. Jonathan smiled shyly and Laura grabbed her hand.

'Daddy's got you a present,' said Debbie.

'Shut up!' said Jonathan. 'It's a surprise!'

Behind them, coming up the stairs came Francis with a sheaf of flowers in one hand and a box of chocolates in the other.

'Can I open the chocolates and share them out?' asked Laura.

The whole family burst out laughing, and to the sound of merry chuckles, they all thronged downstairs.

[1] Joel 2:21

CHAPTER TWENTY-NINE

THE DARK NIGHT OF THE SOUL

There is in God, some say
A deep, but dazzling darkness: as
  men here
Say it is late and dusky, because
  they
See not all clear.
O, for that night! When I in him
Might live invisible and dim.

Night
Henry Vaughan

THE CROSS BEHIND BARS continued to surprise the Proctors and Jenny. It stayed near the top of the Christian bestseller list for several months. Many prison officers walked the half mile from Strangeways to W. H. Smiths in the Arndale Centre and bought a copy. The Prison Officers' official newspaper printed the whole of the last chapter about the cell fires. Noel was thrilled by the reception his book had among the staff as well as the prisoners. 'I thought people would think I was a bit strange in the book,' he said to Jenny. 'That it would put them off me.' He shook his head and smiled. 'But it's had the opposite effect! So many Officers have come up to me and shaken me by the hand and said it's all made them think! I'm amazed! I really am!'

One Saturday morning a *Manchester Evening News* editor rang Jenny up and asked her about the book.

She told him the story.

He cleared his throat.

She said, 'I'm surprised myself that it's doing so well. I didn't know so many people would buy a religious book. It's already into its fourth printing!'

He said, 'Do you realize you are talking about a publishing success? Religious or not, that's a rarity these days!'

She said, 'I....'

He said, 'I'll do a report about it.'

'Oh....'

He rang off.

But in the middle of the joy of her book doing so well and her short stories being read out on Radio Manchester and her being invited several times to talk about her Christian experience on Radio Four, when she should have been rejoicing, she found the old darkness and despair edging in on her again.

One day she trailed into the kitchen. She opened a drawer and found some dusters. Then she trudged upstairs. She began to spring-clean her writing desk. First she lifted one file out; then another. She was almost at the bottom of the drawer when suddenly she stopped. The duster fell from her hand. She stared at the last file. She leaned forward and stared hard. Right on top of the last file, hidden there for so many months, was a palm cross. She didn't remember when she'd put it there, but now it lay and stared back, its message eloquent in her heart.

Then she shut the drawer. No, she thought. And shaking her head she retreated from the drawer. She went and looked at herself in the mirror. She'd had enough. Surely now it was time for her to settle back and....

But even before the easier thoughts took over she was adjusting her mind to the old revelation. Slowly she turned away from the looking-glass. She went back to the drawer. She opened it. She bent down and picked up the palm cross. She looked at it in her hand and as she looked she saw that she had to stay on the path she had chosen so long ago. If writing for God was her task, then she knew it meant isolation; loneliness even. It meant some would misunderstand her and not share her vision for books. But she had to walk by faith. She had to trust the Lord, knowing that whatever she did or wrote the shadow of the cross would always be part of it. She picked up the palm cross and put it on her dressing-table where she could see it. Then she turned and set off downstairs again.

At the top of the stairs she stopped. The evening before she had watched a Science programme on BBC2 about the brain. The scientists said they took the view that the brain was like a computer, a machine, programmed by oneself. Now, as she hovered at the head of the staircase, the old-old anguish gripped her. What if, in the end, that were the only truth? That man was a machine, ruled by a computer made up of cells and nerve endings and electrical impulses? That man was a chance thing, going from the dark into the dark?

But even that didn't make sense. For how could she trust her brain to tell her the truth if it were itself a product of chance? And if chance were the only truth—then that fact in itself could not be trusted. She rubbed her aching head. It didn't make sense. She didn't understand. Not at all.

Later she told Francis. He went quiet. She clutched his arm. 'Tell me! Tell me! Do you know any truth? What is the truth?'

He sat for several minutes in complete silence. Then he said, 'Look to Jesus, Jenny. Look to Jesus. He's the only truth I know of.'

That night she tossed and turned. Finally, unable to stand it any more, she crept downstairs and looked at the clock. It was two in the morning. She sighed and turned to go into the kitchen and make a cup of tea, when all at once she stood dead still in the room. The thoughts that had been battling through her mind all day and half the night suddenly threatened to overwhelm her. She stood on and stared straight ahead at their red wall with its shelves of books and the Rembrandt print. She clenched her fists and raised her chin ever so slightly. Every thought, everything she'd learned, of modern writers and artists flooded into her mind. They and the whole thrust of modern civilization were calling to her, calling ever more loudly and ever more insistently: 'Don't believe! Don't believe! Only fools believe in a Christ! There's nothing there. Nothing...Nothing....'

She pursed her lips together and narrowed her eyes. She refused to give ground but stared steadily on in front of her.

'No,' she said finally. 'I will not give in. Even if I'm a fool, I won't.' In a voice louder than she expected she said, 'You darkness you! You all-evil, all pulling-down, defeating, you... I won't give in. I declare war on you. In the name of Jesus of Nazareth I declare war...on all darkness.'

The silence was total.

'Even if it's the end of me, I won't give in. I won't get off my mountain.' She stood on for several moments, then turned for the kitchen. She made the tea, drank it rapidly, climbed the stairs and fell into a dreamless sleep.

But day after day the battle raged in her mind. At last, one morning after she had taken the children to school, she ran upstairs, went in the bedroom and shut the door. Her hands clenched, unclenched and clenched again. 'Oh God!' she cried out. 'Save me from this... this darkness. This fear of death. This terror of falling into Nothing!'

She raised her head. She cried out in another tongue. The unknown word sprang from her lips into the room. Again and again she called out the single word.

All at once she stopped. She put her hand to her mouth. She remembered.... Quickly she grabbed her Bible. She fumbled with the pages. And then, at last, at last there it was! She read and reread the words revealed to St John:

> The bottomless pit! The Abyss! The bottomless pit!'[1]

She looked in Matthew's Gospel. She read the words of Jesus:

> Outer darkness! Outer darkness! Outer darkness![2]

She stood still and stared unseeingly in front of her. The fear of 'Nothing' quite suddenly grew small. It took its place. For it had been known about and written about in the Bible. It existed. It was not the whole story. It had a Prince. But he was not the King and he did not reign. She knew she didn't fully understand. But one thing was for sure. Her shoulders relaxed, as if a great burden had fallen from them. She had dwelled in a land of darkness. But now she had seen a great light. And she knew. The darkness could not put it out.

[1]Revelation 9:11; 11:7; 17:8; 20:1–3.
[2]Matthew 8:12; 22:13; 25:30.

CHAPTER THIRTY

JESUS, LOVER OF MY SOUL

Sometimes the Lord does not send a person to tell the Good News in a foreign land. He asks them to explore the dark continent within their own mind. To bring the light of Christ to each place of shadows. To risk asking Jesus to set them free from their own bondage to sin, suffering and fear of death. To dare to come out of their prison and have their broken hearts bound up by the one who is light. To discover for once and for all that the darkness cannot put out the light.

Then, and only then, can they share the Good News with their own people.

The Africa Within
Jenny Cooke, 1984

JENNY WALKED UP the pathway to the church in Didsbury and slipped through the door. Quietly she joined in the service. She listened as David Hallatt preached. She closed her eyes as Nick Barker prayed. Then, when the time came, she went and stood with the leaders and the few others behind the communion rail. She bowed her head and waited.

People were coming forward, kneeling, receiving communion, remembering the Lord's death and resurrection for all time...she stood back, silently waiting as the church leaders murmured the age-old words of truth and gave out the bread and the wine.

Some of the people lingered and indicated they'd like the laying-on of hands.

'I've been ill...please help me.'

'I've lost my job. I'm depressed....'

'My friend at work's in hospital. I'm worried about him.'

'I need new inspiration for my work.'

'My back hurts.'

'My boyfriend's left me.'

'I want to give thanks....'

When it was Jenny's turn she stood with the vicar and together they listened, prayed and laid hands on person by person. As they did so Jenny felt her heart begin to beat faster. Then it seemed to grow bigger and bigger until her chest hurt. A love so joyous, so golden, so immense, poured into her for each person as they came and laid down their burden at the feet of their Lord.

'He loves you,' she said. 'He loves you. Loves you.'

The sense of his presence became like a mighty wind,

contained within the frailty of her body. So she stood quite still except for the quivering in her hands.

Later, after the last one had gone back to their seat, she slipped silently away and sat quietly on her own. Her body ached with the weight of the Lord's presence, his power, his love. Slowly, ever so slowly, the weight of love receded. She leaned her forehead against the cool pew in front and found her knees were trembling. She knew she was afraid of what had happened to her. Afraid. It was almost too much to bear...but no. Fear was the wrong word. It was...awe. Awe at the terror of goodness.

Then one dark January morning a few weeks later, she invited her friend Sue round for coffee. They had shared so much over the years, from being girls together at University talking of Vietnam, to the present, both women with children of their own.

Jenny stared at Sue as they sat by the fire. 'But what did it mean, Sue? I just don't understand it!' And she shook her head.

Sue said, 'But don't you understand, Jenny? That joy you felt. That love you had when you saw the people walking up to the communion rail, asking for healing and forgiveness. Don't you see? That was God. You touched God. That's how he feels about us.'

Jenny stared at her blankly.

Sue said, 'That's what is at the centre of the universe. It's love. A God, a personality who is love. He touched you. You felt him. You knew. And that's what it's all about.'

'You mean...? But it was so real!'

Sue said, 'He is real. The most real thing in the world. Only often we don't see it. We don't feel him.'

Jenny looked up. 'You mean what I felt for those few minutes was really him? But....'

Sue smiled gently. 'He can't die again,' she said. 'That's what we believe.'

When Sue had gone Jenny sat on by the fire. She remembered that afternoon years before when God had called her to give up the four things: her writing, her English teaching, her trip to America and her fiancé. It had been hard, bitterly hard. Yet now as she looked back over the years since then she saw that each of those things had been given back to her. Not meagrely, but a hundred times more.

As she warmed her hands by the fire she saw that she had a story to tell. And her story had a beginning and a middle, and, she knew, would have an end. With a quickening of breath she saw that a story presupposed meaning. Stories without meaning did not have beginnings, and middles with emerging patterns, unfolding events and things given back a hundred times as much.

She looked back over her life and saw the narrow path she had travelled winding over, as it were, a vista of mountains. She had been in the valley of humiliation and despair. She had struggled up peaks and found new joys and understanding. On the dark side of one mountain she had caught a sudden glimpse of the redemptive power of God, taking away only to give back more. He did not only forgive people their sins and fit them for a future heaven, he remade them now, from the inside out. She thought of herself as she might have been. No! As she would have been. And she saw with wonder, that she was different now. She was changed.

All at once, with a surge of joy, she realized that true meaning in life did not lie, in the end, with a satisfactory system of thought, even though that was an important peg for people to hang understanding on. Meaning lay in a person, in love, in relationships. And true meaning lay in a relationship with Jesus Christ.

A question formed in her mind. But even before she had time to ask it she knew the answer. God had allowed her to feel and know the darkness as she had, so that she could understand the anguish of modern man. She was identified with her generation as they searched and searched for meaning. She bowed her head. Perhaps, just perhaps, she might have to go that way again.

Then one morning as she lay awake in the half light she found herself thinking about her dark night of the soul and it troubled her. The hour ticked by and the sorrow did not lift.

All at once there came a whisper, a hint of a voice so still and so small that she half turned her head to catch the words. 'But didn't you know that I am with you?' came the voice.

She lay very still. She knew that voice.

'Had you forgotten that I am with you?'

She closed her eyes. She couldn't see him, but he was so close he could almost be in her blind spot.

'I am with you. I have been with you all the time. All the way over those mountains. All the way in the pain. All the way out of the pain. I will never fail you, nor forsake you. I will be with you all the way into the future. And beyond the future.'

Jesus, she thought. Lover of my soul.

'Had you forgotten? I am with you wherever you go. I am your shield and your exceeding great reward. It is I.'

So that was the meaning of her life. Her search was to find her Lord and to be found by him. And when she died and met him face to face she wouldn't need to be afraid because she would be meeting someone she had known for a very long time.

'I am with you,' came the whisper again. 'I am with you. With you.'

She lay back and shut her eyes. Joy surged in her mind. At last she had understood.

The Cross Behind Bars

The true story of Noel Proctor—
Prison Chaplain

by Jenny Cooke

As a boy, Noel Proctor thought that God didn't live outside the Sunday School classroom. Until something happened that was to turn his life upside down and launch him into a totally unexpected career: chaplain to one of Her Majesty's prisons.

Noel soon discovered that he couldn't convert the hardened inmates of Britain's prisons singlehanded. God had to do a deeper work in his life before revival could come to the nation's 'forgotten people'.

This is the warm and intimate account of how one man learned to live in the power and will of God, and how his wife found the courage to fight 'terminal' cancer. Above all it shows how God's power can be released when his people put him first in their lives.

Noel Proctor *held chaplaincies at Wandsworth, Eastchurch and Dartmoor Prisons before becoming Senior Chaplain at Strangeways in Manchester.*

Jenny Cooke *is an adult education tutor who teaches creative writing. She is married with three children.*

Kingsway Publications